IDTRAVELLING

The Best Book to Read on a Plane

Funny Travel Stories, Interesting Facts About Airplanes and Airports, Bizarre Laws, and Customs From Around the World That Will Make Your Flight More Entertaining

ID travelling

First published by IDtravelling 2021

First edition

ISBN: 978-1-9994579-1-4

This book was professionally typeset on Reedsy.
Find out more at reedsy.com

Contents

1

Introduction

"Make sure your seat backs and tray tables are in their full upright position and that your seat belt is correctly fastened. Also, your portable electronic devices must be set to 'airplane' mode until an announcement is made upon arrival. Thank you." This is a typical airplane announcement you hear during takeoff. Its meaning may differ depending on the passengers. For some, it means they will be able to see friends or family members who live overseas and whom they haven't seen in a while. For others, it means the beginning of a big adventure. No matter what it may mean, this announcement also means you still have a few hours until you reach your destination. Until you do, this book will make your flight a bit more interesting.

One chapter in this book discusses myths surrounding air travel. The chapter presents different statements; some are true, others are false. Here is an example. Is the following statement a myth? "Airlines can ask you to present a credit card at check-in after you purchased the ticket online." This statement is true. Some airlines have a policy of asking travelers to present a credit card at check-in and denying boarding to passengers who cannot prove they have purchased the ticket. This measure is designed to prevent fraudulent purchases. It is more likely that airlines will ask to present a credit card when none of the passengers' names match the name on the credit card used to purchase the tickets. Another reason is when the credit card used for purchase has expired or was canceled before the check-in. Therefore, when purchasing a ticket online with a credit card, it is preferable that the name on the card matches one of the passenger names. And, the best thing to do is to check the policy of the airline you are traveling with, especially in special cases like when using your credit card to purchase a ticket for someone else who is traveling without you. Checking credit cards at check-in is more common in Asia and the Middle East than in North America.

Myths about air travel only make up one chapter of this book. There is much more exciting and useful information in this book, like customs and rules from around the world, funny travel stories, and travel-related trivia. Let's take off.

2

Pre-flight

Travel does not begin when you get on the plane; it starts months before. When you book your flight, you envision what places you will see, what food you will eat, and what experiences you will encounter. It is also an excellent time to prepare for your flight. You probably know the following information if you have flown before, but it is worth repeating. To travel internationally, you will need a valid passport. A common rule for passport validity is the six-month validity rule, which states that travelers' passports should be valid six months after leaving a chosen destination. Some countries won't let travelers in if their passports expire in less than six months, so it is a good idea to check for passport validity rules in your destination.

Another essential thing to do when preparing for a flight is to label your suitcases. Although airlines losing luggage is becoming less common, it still happens, which is the primary reason to add a luggage tag. Should the luggage be found, the owner can easily be contacted. It is important to provide contact information so that you can be contacted but at the same time not provide too much information for privacy reasons. Many people within an airport can see your luggage tag. Thus, it is advisable to avoid writing your home phone number and home address to reduce the risk of home burglary while you are away.

A common practice is to put the following information on the luggage tag:

- Name and surname, with the first name shortened to one letter.
- Email address; use a secondary email address to avoid phishing attempts on your primary one.
- Mobile phone number with the proper country and area code.

If you don't want to write any private information on the tag, you can use a smart tag. There are different types of smart luggage tags. Some contain a QR code and a web address. The owner's contact information can be obtained by scanning the code or navigating to the web address. Also, it is recommended to take a photo of your luggage and tag so you will have proof they are yours. Finally, remove any stickers from previous travels. Old stickers can cause confusion if they are read in place of the current trip's stickers.

Occasionally, when flights are full, baggage space quickly runs out onboard as earlier boarding classes finish storing their luggage. Should space run out, you will be required to check your bag for storage below. It is essential to tag your carry-on bag as well in case another passenger picks it up on their way off the plane, it gets lost in the airport, or if you're asked to check it on board. Place a second tag containing the same pertinent information inside the suitcases. This way, there will always be a backup.

Packing the correct items in your carry-on bag can make a significant impact on your flight. Of course, all items should pass through airport security and be allowed on the plane. When packing your carry-on, it is important to remember that checked luggage sometimes gets lost. There is a possibility you will spend a few days at the destination without it. Airlines losing luggage is not very common nowadays. Airlines lose about 2 bags for every 1,000 passengers on average, including temporary and permanent luggage loss. Here is a list of items that are worth packing in the carry-on to make a flight more comfortable and entertaining:

Daily over-the-counter medications such as pain relievers you might need during your flight.

- Electronic devices (phone, gaming systems, or eReaders) and their charging cords.
- Things to keep you or children traveling with you occupied (such as portable games or coloring books).
- Magazines or books to read ("The Best Book to Read on a Plane" is recommended).
- Any expensive items that you want to keep an eye on.
- Documents like tickets to events, directions to the hotel, and reservations. It is better to print those rather than having them only as a digital version.
- A change of clothes, including underwear.

- A toothbrush, toothpaste, and any essential hygiene supplies (like feminine products).
- Small snacks such as a bag of pretzels or chips.

3

Terminal Boredom

You know this feeling, sitting in the airport waiting for your flight. Staring at the clock. Staring at your phone. Watching the gate agent. Watching people walk by. It seems to take forever for your flight to board. You are looking at the airport codes displayed on the flight information display system (FIDS). Some codes like JFK (John F. Kennedy International Airport in New York) and SFO (San Francisco International Airport) make sense because you can associate the letters with the airport or city name. Others, you kind of know but are not sure about a particular letter—for example, LAX (Los Angeles International Airport). LA letters are clear, but where does the X come from? Also, some airport codes have letters that have nothing to do with the airport or city name—for example, YYZ (Pearson International Airport in Toronto). An airport code or IATA (International Air Transport Association) airport code is a three-letter geocode designating many airports around the world. In the past, pilots in the United States used two-letter codes to identify cities but later moved to a three-letter identification. With the number of airports worldwide, two-letter codes wouldn't be enough to provide each airport with a unique letter combination. With two letters, there are a total of 676 permutations if using only 26 Latin letters. However, with three letters, there are 17,576 permutations.

There are over 9,000 IATA location codes in use. Generally, airport codes are selected as a combination of the letters in the airport or city name, like ATL (Atlanta), SIN (Singapore), or HKG (Hong Kong). Some airport codes in the United States use the two letters pilots had used in the past with an "X" at the end, like LAX or PDX (Portland). In Canada, most large airports have codes that begin with the letter "Y" followed by two letters in the city's name, like YOW (Ottawa) and YVR (Vancouver). There are exceptions to this rule—Canada's largest airport, Toronto Pearson Airport, has the code YYZ. What's the takeaway? There are different historical and geographical reasons affecting airport codes.

To conclude, airport codes are not always intuitive. How well do you know airport codes? At the end of this book, you will find the Trivia chapter where your knowledge about "Everything Travel," including airport codes, will be tested. IATA codes are also used to identify train stations and locations like cities. Large metropolitan areas that have several airports can have their own codes. For example, the code NYC is assigned to New York City and not to a specific airport. It can be helpful when searching online for a flight to New York. By inserting the code NYC in the destination field, a search is conducted, including all airports in New York. IATA also provides 2-letter airline codes. There are over 1,000 assigned airline codes.

While sitting and waiting for your flight, you are getting hungry and decide to grab a bite to eat. You buy a sandwich and realize that it is significantly more expensive than a similar sandwich outside the airport. Food and drinks at airports can be twice as expensive as outside. You might think they can charge so much just because people are stuck inside the terminal and cannot leave to buy food. However, there are a few other reasons why airport food is expensive. The first reason relates to inventory control. All inventory must pass through security, significantly slowing down the pace of goods reaching the business' stockroom. Yes, your overpriced fish and chips were looked over to ensure the packages of frozen food didn't contain contraband. Another reason for expensive airport food relates to staffing. Staff members, especially new staff, must jump through hoops to get to work, depending on the airport. They must pay for their own parking, and go through security, just as a passenger would. Airports offer security passes for their employees, allowing them to walk through screening faster. However, the processing times can be high. Employers also face higher wage bills, as many airport jobs are unionized, costing $2 more per hour for a position inside the airport than outside.

A little more broke but full, you return to your seat by the gate. Scanning social media on your phone, dealing with the airport's poor Wi-Fi signal, you wonder, "Who owns this place, and how does this place make money?" Most US commercial airports are owned and operated by public entities, including local, regional, or state governments. As to income, airport incomes vary but can broadly be split into two categories. The first category is Commercial-Support. In the largest airports, most revenue comes from charging airline carriers for lane usage and charging rent from vendors and restaurants within the airport. Some airports, especially smaller airports in rural communities, are mainly supported through government funding. They lack the customer volume to charge carriers for lane usage or shops and restaurants to charge rent. In a large, regional airport, over 50% of all income is made through charging airlines lane usage. Over 40% is derived from rent charges to restaurants and vendors, and less than 5% is derived from government support.

Getting bored, you pull out your ticket and start scanning it over, double-checking everything over once more. Are you going to the correct location? Are you at the right gate? You compare your ticket against the board at the gate, matching up the destination and flight number. Everything is still good to go. Time continues to tick by, and you're getting even more bored by the second. You still have a few hours to go. If you're lucky enough to be in some of the following airports, you just might have something interesting to do.

Are you a golf fan? A United States Golf Association (USGA)-approved nine-hole golf course, open to travelers, is located by Terminal 2 of Hong Kong International Airport. At San Francisco and Chicago Midway airports, you can find in-airport yoga rooms with provided mats. Are you at Amsterdam Schiphol Airport and in an arty mood? Check out an extension of the Rijksmuseum, one of the world's most famous European art museums. Need cleaning or got a toothache? In Terminal 2 of the Sao Paulo airport, you can see an in-house dentist. You can drink anywhere on the property in the Nashville airport as the airport possesses a liquor license. No more being tied to the bar. At JFK, winter travel has just become easier! JFK features a coat-check, allowing flyers to check their coat in for extended periods of time, only to pick it back upon return to the airport—an excellent option for those taking a winter vacation to the tropics. The coat-check even gives the option to keep track of your garment via an interactive app. Coat-check is also available in other airports worldwide, especially in cities with cold winters, so travelers can leave their coats when traveling to warm destinations. Changi Airport in Singapore features a nature trail that is home to over 1,000 butterflies. Some airports, including Tokyo's Narita International Airport and Kuala Lumpur International Airport (KLIA), have capsule hotels where you can take a nap.

Departure is slowly getting closer! Did you remember to visit the bathroom before boarding? Going to the toilet before boarding is important because the bathroom on the plane can be busy during boarding and cannot be used during takeoff. So, it might take a while until you can use it.

Finally! You've been called to board. You get your ticket out, gather your things, and head for the line formed at the gate counter. It is time to get started on your next grand adventure.

4

Flight Myths

The world of air travel has many interesting facts to offer. It is also filled with myths. We will learn a bit more about air travel and will see some air travel myths. Listed below are statements about air travel and an explanation of whether they are true or false.

Pilots use a key to start a plane, similar to starting a car

False (mostly). A key may be required to start the engine in some small aircraft. However, large commercial airplanes don't have ignition keys. Instead, to turn on a commercial aircraft, pilots operate a series of buttons that switch on different aircraft systems.

Pilots eat different meals during the flight

True. While the rule varies between airlines, most pilots are given the multi-course first-class meal served to passengers. At the same time, the co-pilots must eat meals from the menus of the other classes on the flight. While this seems cruel, it is actually a safety measure. The reason pilots eat different meals is to reduce the risk of both having food poisoning.

You need to be on a business trip to fly in business class

False. Business class is one of the more expensive classes. You can fly business if you want and can afford it. You don't have to be a businessperson or on a business trip.

Food tastes different in the air

True. If you ever felt like the taste of food in the air differs from on the ground, you were not mistaken. It is estimated that the sensitivity of taste buds to sweet and salty is reduced by around 30% during a flight. This phenomenon is attributed to the difference in air pressure along with the low humidity in a plane's cabin. These changes make it more difficult for your taste buds to sense sweet and salty flavors.

You cannot open and drink your booze on the plane

True. You cannot bring out your own alcohol and start drinking on the plane. However, some airlines allow their cabin crew members to serve passengers alcohol they brought. If you ask a cabin crew member to serve you the alcohol you've brought, and they agree to, you can drink it. However, at the end of the flight, the crew member will have to throw away the open bottle, finished or not. So, if you plan to bring a bottle, a good idea will be to get a small bottle that you can finish during a flight.

If you're born on a flight, you get free flights for life on the airline on which flight you were born.

False (mostly). Unfortunately for future babies born on flights, they are not guaranteed free flights for life like this myth indicates. Having said that, some babies born on flights have been awarded free flights for life by their respective airlines. In other words, a baby will be provided with free flights for life only if it is the airline policy. Each airline sets its own guidelines for how late into term pregnant passengers can fly. Typically, airlines won't allow pregnant passengers to fly when they are close to the due date. The specific number of weeks before the due date depends on airline policies. So it is unlikely for a baby to be born on a flight.

In airplanes, there is a mechanism for pilots to flush the sewage tank mid-flight

False. Airlines are not allowed to dump their waste tanks in mid-flight. Planes can't drop human waste based on a pilot decision. There is no "button" on the dashboard to do so. Instead, toilet waste is stored in a tank during a flight and emptied at the airport after the plane has landed.

Pilots have parachutes

False. While it is true that specific aircraft, such as military-grade fighters, do have parachutes, passenger planes do not. Pilots do not have parachutes, as it is their job to safely land the aircraft in an emergency, not make a quick escape.

Commercial planes sometimes fly with only one pilot

False. There are at least two pilots on commercial airlines, and on some flights, there are three. There are some exceptions to this rule, like in small private jets that a single pilot can operate. But even in private jets, there are usually two pilots. There is a captain and a first officer (or a pilot and a co-pilot), and the captain usually has more seniority. Having more than one pilot is a great safety measure that allows a proper operation of the plane in case one pilot cannot operate it for some reason.

Airplanes have secret rooms for pilots and cabin crew

True. On many planes that service long-haul routes, there are compartments, usually above first class, containing small rooms for the cabin crew to rest between their shifts. While the rooms are incredibly basic, they do feature beds and, on some planes, entertainment systems.

Airplanes have horns

True. Airplanes have horns, but they are used for different purposes than horns in cars. While in cars, horns are used for warning, horns in planes are mainly used as a communication method and provide ground engineers with information about the status of the airplane's systems. The horn can only be used on the ground since it doesn't work when it is in flight.

Airlines make small profits from selling tickets

True. Although flight prices may seem high, the profit a sold ticket generates for the airline can be low because of high expenses like airport fees, fuel, and flight crew. For tickets that go for a few hundred dollars, an airline's profit can be as low as $20 per passenger on average. However, selling tickets is not the only way airlines make money. They also generate income from associated fees like baggage, seat, and reservation-change fees. With enough passenger traffic, associated fees can turn into a significant income. Also, tickets in the more premium cabins like first and business generate more profit than the less expensive ones like economy. Sometimes, low-fare tickets don't cover the airline's cost, but airlines prefer them over empty seats that don't bring any money.

5

Welcome Aboard

Your boarding number is called. You join the line, have your ticket scanned, and head down the gangway toward the plane, the hum of the engines filling the air. As you board, a flight attendant stationed at the door will welcome you aboard. Have you ever felt strange when entering a plane and crew members were smiling, greeting, and looking at you? The truth is, they are not only there to welcome you aboard. As everyone enters the plane, flight attendants have been trained to visually scan you down to check for potential issues during the flight. This could be spotting someone who is drunk and may cause problems. There have been cases where drunk passengers were spotted by flight attendants and weren't allowed on a flight due to safety concerns. The crew also looks for someone who looks sickly, passengers with disabilities who may require assistance or muscular passengers who may assist during the flight with tasks requiring physical strength. Don't forget to greet the crew back and be nice to the crew during the flight. Being a flight attendant is demanding. Help them do their job better by being polite, paying attention to the safety demonstration, and listening to other things they ask you to do.

As you enter the plane, a flight attendant will recheck your ticket. It will have your row number and seat letter printed somewhere along the top. For example, "47A." Have you ever noticed that a seat with the letter "I" is missing? It is because the letter "I" looks like the number "1" and can confuse. Airlines also avoid using O and S letters for seats because they look like numbers. You file down the rows, through first and business class, and keep your eyes peeled to either side. Once you've arrived at your seat, stow your carry-on either into the overhead rack or underneath the seat in front of you. Remember, there are other people behind you still filing onto the plane. If you're having difficulties, step into your row to allow others to pass as you sort out the problem. Remember not to fight the flow of traffic. For complex situations like when another passenger has the same seat as you on their boarding pass, head to the back of the plane for assistance from a flight attendant.

Since you are stuck on an airplane with other people, it is helpful to know flight etiquette rules. Here are some of them that can make the flight more enjoyable for yourself and other passengers. The first one is reclining. It is best to avoid reclining if possible because it can cause discomfort for the person sitting behind you. If you do recline, for example, to be in a more comfortable position for sleep, recline as little as you can. Do it slowly so you won't hurt anyone or anything behind you. Also, avoid reclining during meal times.

Do you talk to strangers on a flight? Many people avoid talking to strangers on flights. However, studies have shown that those who speak to strangers can receive a slight boost in happiness and productivity. Perhaps you should change your mind about not speaking to your seatmates? However, if your seat partner seems unwilling to talk, don't press them.

During a flight, there are specific times when plane window shades should be raised or lowered. They should be raised during takeoff and landing and lowered when passengers sleep like in red-eye flights. But, who decides if they should be raised or lowered during other times? It is primarily considered the right of the window-seat holder to determine if the shade is raised or lowered. If you aren't in the window seat, feel free to ask to have it raised or lowered, but also be prepared to be declined. If you are in the window seat, be aware of others in your row—for example, if people want to see the view below or if a child wants to see out the window.

Many people prefer to take their shoes off during a flight for comfort. If you choose to take your shoes off, it is suggested that you take a pair of slippers with you in your carry-on to change into. Since airplanes are used by so many people, it is safe to assume that some surfaces are not spectacularly clean, such as the floor and seat trays. Thus, you probably don't want your socks to touch the floor.

Upon landing, you might hear people clapping. Some people clap because they are happy to be on the ground again. Others clap after a particularly bumpy flight. For some, clapping is a way to express gratitude to the flight crew. Some people are averse to clapping. According to them, we don't clap for cab drivers or baristas; there is no need to clap for the pilots and cabin crew. There is neither a consensus among the airplane crew. When one retired airline captain was asked what he thought about the clapping, he said that it always made him smile that passengers show appreciation by clapping. According to a different source, some pilots don't like people clapping because landing correctly is their job. Since there is no rule or agreement, passengers can do what their hearts desire when it comes to landing clapping.

A book about air travel wouldn't be complete without mentioning jet lag. Jet lag is the body's response to a quick change in time zones—the larger the gap, the larger the bodily reaction. Common symptoms include disorientation, irritability, insomnia, fatigue, dry eyes, and headaches. There are traditional ways to prevent or reduce jet lag's effect. These ways include preparing your body before the flight with exercise, keeping hydrated, and having a good night's sleep. Also, during the flight, sleeping enough when arriving in the morning, staying hydrated, and avoiding caffeine or alcohol will help you fight off jet lag.

There are also non-traditional ways to fight jet lag. One of these ways we found online was titled "the cabin crew's secret to avoiding jet lag." In this article, a flight attendant shared her tip for not getting jet lag on long-haul flights—simply not eating. According to her, she was advised that the human digestive system nearly "shuts down" at high altitudes, making it better to simply not eat while in the air. She mentioned that eating during a flight causes the digestive system to work extra hard after landing, which makes you more tired. Instead, it is best to drink plenty of water and stay hydrated, and have a meal once on land again.

On the one hand, this tip comes from a flight attendant who flies all the time and should know how to deal with jet lag. On the other hand, some flights are very long. For example, a flight from Singapore to Newark, New Jersey, can last over 18 hours. It is hard to imagine not eating for over 18 hours. Also, it might be dangerous for some people.

6

Flight Questions Answered

What are the tiny circles in the plane window? Do flight attendants really get free flights? Is it a good idea to drink airplane coffee? These and other questions will be answered in this chapter.

Why the classes? Why the price difference?

There can be five classes on large flights. Different airlines have different names for their classes, but they are generally identified as first, business, and various types of economy—basic economy, economy, premium economy. For example, a one-way direct flight from New York to London can cost $819 in basic economy and $12,884 in first class. So what are the differences between the classes? Here are some general differences regarding seat area, meals, and overall comfort. More airline-specific differences can usually be found on the airline website.

First class (most expensive)

In the old days of flying, all seats were first class. However, as airlines strived to make air travel accessible for all and airplane seat capacities grew larger, economy seats came to call. In first class, you'll get priority boarding, an extra checked bag, the largest seat sizes on the plane, and, depending on the carrier, free drinks (including alcohol) and better food service. Most also come with an amenities kit for overnight flights.

Business class

Think of business as first-class light. These seats are also large (but sometimes not as large as in first class) and feature upgraded dining and amenities onboard. Some airlines have eliminated first class, combining the two together. Business class originated in the late 1970s when there was a demand by business people to fly in a class that is quieter and more spacious than economy class, which was often full of noisy families but not as expensive as first class. This class was initially designed as an intermediate level of service between economy and first class. Did you know that there is such a thing as a business-class airline? It is an airline that has only one class on its flights. You probably guessed it—it is business class.

Economy class

Economy class will vary, but generally, boards before basic economy class, and includes a checked bag and the ability to choose your seat.

Basic economy class

This class offers the least level of amenities as well as the smallest seat capacity. However, this class is known for cheap fares for those looking to get to their destination quickly on a smaller budget.

How is it possible to receive warm food in the air? How is the food warmed up?

Surprisingly, the technology does not differ from something you may have in your kitchen—convection ovens. The pre-prepared trays, brought in each flight by the prep crew, are simply piled into convection ovens and heated for about twenty minutes before serving. Unfortunately, you probably won't find a chef in the back prepping your meal—it is all done in industrial kitchens contracted out by the airline.

Is it a good idea to drink airplane coffee?

Research and maintenance statistics have proven that drinking the "tap" water from an airplane is not a good idea. While the freshwater tanks of planes are cleaned, they are not emptied and cleaned "routinely." Therefore, bacteria have time to grow between cleanings. Consequently, it is best to drink only bottled or canned drinks on a flight and not tap water, including warm beverages like tea or coffee.

What are the tiny circles in the plane window?

The tiny hole in the window, also called a "bleed hole," is designed to balance air pressure. The pressure inside the plane is maintained, so it is at a safe level, but the pressure outside is dropped the higher the plane gets. This creates a big difference between the pressure inside and outside the aircraft, leading to increased physical stress on airplane windows. Therefore, the airplane window comprises three panes. The bleed hole takes the pressure off the inner pane and transfers it to the outer pane. The middle pane acts as a fail-safe.

What are some interesting flight facts?

- According to data from 2017, an estimate of more than 9,500 planes, carrying over 1.27 million people, are in the sky at any given time.
- According to data from January 2020, the busiest commercial route is actually a domestic route in South Korea between Gimpo Airport in Seoul to Jeju island. Every year, over 13 million people fly this route. With up to 180 daily flights, this translates to an average of a flight every 8 minutes. Why are so many people flying to Jeju island? It is a popular holiday destination that attracts many tourists thanks to its weather, nature, and beaches. The busiest domestic route in the US is Los Angeles to San Francisco, with over 35,300 annual flights, which is over 95 daily flights on average. The busiest international route is between Kuala Lumpur and Singapore, with over 30,000 annual flights.
- The average flight travels at 35,000 feet (6.63 miles / 10.67 km). It usually reaches its cruising altitude in the first 10 minutes of the flight.
- Commercial planes' flight speed is about 550 miles per hour (885 km per hour).
- An estimated 38.9 million aircraft departures occurred in 2019.

Why are some seats marked with a triangle?

These triangles are markers for the flight crew to show the window with the best view of the wings, should they need to look at them.

Who is the world's most frequent flyer?

In 2019, Tom Stuker set the world's record at 21 million miles flown. The married father of three from New Jersey says he's simply addicted to flying, but don't worry, his wife often flies with him. Also, Tom pays for his flights out-of-pocket. The miles he earns he gives to charities, family, and others.

Why are most aircraft painted white?

Although each airline has a unique livery, the predominant color on planes is usually white. There are several safety and cost reasons to use white. First, damages such as corrosion, rust spots, and oil spills will be easier to spot on a white airplane. Therefore, it is easier to fix. Second, the white color does not fade as fast as other colors, meaning that the aircraft has to be repainted less frequently. Third, airlines and leasing companies often sell their planes to other carriers. By keeping the main body white, it is less expensive to change the livery. Finally, white paint helps reflect sunlight and reduce the amount of energy required to keep an aircraft at a comfortable temperature.

How much do flight attendants work? Do they really get free flights?

Flight attendants usually do not have a schedule like most of us nine-to-fivers do. Instead, they "bid" each month on their schedules, with the most senior members selecting first, then trickling down. Many flight attendants will prefer to go for long-haul flights, as they are the most highly paid routes. Why? It's an industry standard that airlines pay for the time spent in the air. This means that a flight attendant is not technically being paid for any time spent on the ground in situations such as waiting for a delayed flight or preparing for a flight.

The number of hours flight attendants work can vary from one month to another. According to the Bureau of Labor Statistics, flight attendants' schedules are anywhere from 75 to 100 hours a month in the air. Making their actual time on the clock around 125-150 hours in total, accounting for on-the-ground time. There are days when flight attendants are on call and can be asked to come to work in the middle of the night. Also, flight attendants work on holidays, especially those who don't have seniority. Flight attendants' job is demanding, and training to become a flight attendant is not easy either. They learn to provide first aid and how to evacuate a plane full of passengers in the most efficient way. People often consider them as servers, while in reality, they are trained professionals whose main objective is to keep you safe. Remember this the next time a flight attendant asks you to buckle your seat belt.

Being a flight attendant has its perks, like visiting many countries and exploring different cultures. Also, flight attendants can get their hands on free or highly discounted flights. While you may initially be jealous of this sweet deal, know that it can come with caveats. Traditionally, these hard-to-come-by passes are "standby tickets." Meaning that attendants and their friends and family may fill a seat if not taken by a paying passenger. If a paying passenger comes along, they are out of luck.

7

Chopsticks User Manual

Different countries have different rules and customs. Often, tourists are not aware of these and can find themselves in awkward situations. Here are some rules and customs from around the world. Since rules constantly change, it's worth checking before your trip for current rules and customs in the country you are visiting.

Japan has different customs that were developed during its long history. Many rules are surrounding eating in general and using chopsticks in particular. How many rules can be around two wooden or plastic sticks? Quite a few, it turns out. Here are some. The first one is rubbing your wooden chopsticks against each other to remove splinters. It could be interpreted that you believe that the wooden chopsticks provided by the restaurant are of inferior quality. Also, no chopstick to chopstick action is allowed. If you'd like to share a taste of your food, place it down onto a plate and allow your meal-sharing partner to take it from there. Direct swapping from chopsticks to chopsticks is considered rude.

Both chopsticks should always be used to hold food. You shouldn't use just one to hold food by stabbing it. Many meals in Japan are served with a bowl of rice. It might be tempting to stick your chopsticks into the rice, but this should also be avoided, as it is similar to an action performed during funerals. Chopsticks shouldn't be crossed. Keep them parallel when holding or placing down.

Besides chopsticks etiquette, there are other table manners in Japan. For example, slurping. You might consider slurping rude, but it is encouraged when eating noodle dishes like ramen in Japan. Slurping noodles is a sign of enjoyment, and it improves the taste of the food. The last dining etiquette rule is about serving your own drink. When dining with other people, you should refill the glasses of others but not your own as it is considered rude. Wait for someone else to do so.

Another Japanese custom is about wearing slippers indoors. Private homes and some establishments in Japan require changing from your "outside" shoes to slippers to preserve the cleanliness of your destination. Also, "bathroom slippers" are typical—switch between the two coming in and out of the bathroom. Just as demonstrated by the shoe customs, cleanliness is a way of life in Japan. For example, suppose you're visiting a public bath. In that case, it is essential to shower first to "cleanse" your body before entering a communal bath to prevent contamination. This rule also applies when using a bathtub at home. The bath serves as a place to relax rather than to clean your body. Body cleaning is performed during the shower.

Japan is not the only country with interesting customs. Take Italy, for example. You might have heard that Italians don't drink milk-based coffee drinks like cappuccino after 11 AM. Italians consider milk with coffee a breakfast drink, as milk is said to upset digestion and shouldn't be consumed after a meal. In Egypt, asking for salt to be added to food is a sign of disrespect, as it indicates that the food is bad or off, therefore insulting the chef.

Need to know how to get somewhere in Nicaragua? Follow the lips. It is not customary to point fingers in Nicaraguan culture. Instead, people point with their lips using the "duck" or "kissy" face, tilting the lips in the direction they want to point. In Malaysia, pointing with your index finger is considered to be rude. If you must point to something, it is best to do so with your thumb with other fingers folded, as if giving a "thumbs up." Transit can be hectic, particularly in larger cities. While this tip works around the world, it is especially so in large Canadian cities. Trying to cram yourself into a crowded public transportation car before people exited is considered rude. It is best to stand either left or right of the open door and wait. It is not uncommon to see a line formed at a bus station of people waiting. Once everyone who needs to has exited, get on board.

In South Korea, it is better to avoid using red ink. Red ink has been traditionally used to write the names of dead relatives on the family register. It is now associated with ill will toward an individual, should you write their name in red ink. In Russia, avoid giving someone a bouquet with an even number of flowers, as bouquets with even numbers are reserved for funerals.

8

Traditions and Customs

You've finally made it to your destination—welcome! After the flight, the first thing you probably want to do is have a nice shower or bath to clean yourself and relax. Bathing is done differently in different parts of the world. Let's see bathing traditions from around the world.

The first bathing tradition is the Turkish hammam. Hammams are probably the most thorough experience of any on this list. On entering, you may be given sandals, a wrap-around towel, and a mitt called a keşe used to exfoliate the skin. The bath is separated into three areas. The first room contains hot steam and a large marble stone in the center where attendants scrub down and massage patrons while the patrons lay on the stone. In a second, cooler room, patrons bathe to wash away any leftover grime after their thorough scrubbing, and the third coolest room is for resting.

In some countries, wood plays a vital role in the bathing culture.

Examples are the Russian banya and Finnish sauna. Russian banyas generally include a cold plunge pool and a hot wooden steam room with wooden benches at different heights where bathers can sit or lay. The higher you go, the hotter it gets, with temperatures reaching up to 100°C (212°F). Of course, we can't not mention the famous veniki—birch twigs—which have been popularized in the media with images of bathers being whipped across the back and front with these branches. They are said to open pores and promote circulation.

Similar to the Russian banya's steam room, the Finnish sauna also has a wooden interior. The major difference between the two is that the Finnish sauna has drier air. Finnish saunas can be traced back to at least the 1100s when they were originally heated using wood-burning stoves. They have remained popular in Finland throughout the times, with estimates stating one sauna per every 2-3 people. In the winter, it is common that once a bather is done with their steam, they leap back outside into the cold to cool down. The transition from hot to cold is thought to promote blood circulation. Although, it can also be dangerous.

The Japanese and Koreans use natural elements in their bathing cultures. Onsens are spread all over Japan. They are baths that use the warm water of natural hot springs. Traditionally, onsens were located outdoors, but nowadays, there are many indoor onsen baths. Onsens are documented all the way back to the year 500. Note that nudity is usually required, but you'll appreciate it once you slip into the warm, relaxing waters. In the past, bathing in onsens wasn't gender-separated. However, today most onsens are gender-separated.

Korean jjimjilbangs are spa complexes with steam rooms, hot tubs, massage areas, and showers. Some are open 24 hours and include a place for an overnight stay. Similar to onsens, jjimjilbangs are gender-separated, and bathing is done with no clothes. Korean jjimjilbangs are known to celebrate nature. You'll find elements like clay, jade, and salt, as it is believed that these natural elements carry health-promoting properties.

It is always interesting to see how the same rituals are performed differently by different cultures. For example, wedding ceremonies are performed worldwide, but they are performed differently in different places. Here are some examples of how various ceremonies are conducted in different countries.

It is customary for the best man, or "koumparos," to step up and shave the groom in Greek weddings. Afterward, it is typical for the new mother-in-law to feed the groom honey and almonds. It must be nice. My mother-in-law never fed me honey and almonds. In the Philippines, during the wedding, the newlyweds release a "couple" of white doves, a male and a female, symbolizing marital harmony and peace. At Cuban wedding receptions, if a man dances with the bride, he should pin some money to her dress. This money is put toward the new couple's honeymoon expenses. This tradition is called "money dance," and it is not unique to Cuba. Different variations of the tradition can be found in Poland, Hungary, Nigeria, Mexico, and the Philippines. In Venezuela, if the bride and groom sneak off to party on their own during the reception, don't be surprised—be happy! It is considered good luck for a guest to catch their absence and good luck for the couple if they escape without being noticed.

An Irish bride, while dancing, must keep one foot on the ground—it is said if she doesn't, evil fairies just may sweep her away. German tradition calls for the bride and groom to saw a log in half together. The completion of this task is said to prove to the crowd that the two will be able to work through problems together in the future. In Romania, all in good fun, members of the wedding party may sweep the bride away to a secret location and demand a ransom from the groom. The groom will have to pay up this sometimes embarrassing fee to get his bride back, but hopefully, singing a song in front of the entire wedding party won't be too bad. The groom may find his tie cut up in Spain, or the bride may find her garters cut up. No, this isn't some ghastly accident, but a fun tradition carried out by the wedding party. The cut-up garments will be sold to members of the wedding to raise some extra money for the couple.

A wedding is a significant event in a couple's lives. Another major event for couples is a child's birth. Similarly to weddings, childbirth traditions vary from country to country. In Israel, brit milah is a common ritual. According to Jewish tradition, eight days after a male child is born, he is circumcised and named in a traditional rite called brit milah. This tradition is not unique to Israel. It is a Jewish ritual that is performed in Jewish communities around the world. In Bali, the placenta is considered a living being worthy of respect. After birth, the placenta is cleaned up, placed in a coconut, and buried outside. In Japan, after the mother and baby are released from the hospital, it is customary for mother and child to recuperate in her parents' home. There, the new mom can rest for about a month, bonding with her child as the family helps with chores. It is common to bring a gift when visiting a newborn. However, in Brazil, it is also customary for a new mom to give visitors small gifts during their visit as gratitude for their visit.

Before traveling abroad, you most likely won't be able to learn a new language to communicate freely. But, you can learn how to say "cheers." Here are some examples:

Chinese
Gān bēi
Pronunciation–Gan bay!

Dutch
Skål
Pronunciation–Skoal!

French
Santé!
Pronunciation–Sahn-tay!

German
Prost / Zum wohl
Pronunciation–Prohst! / Tsum vohl!

Greek
ΥΓΕΙΑ
Pronunciation–Yamas!

Hawaiian
Å'kålè ma'luna
Pronunciation–Okole maluna!

Italian

Salute / Cin cin

Pronunciation–Saw-lutay! / Chin chin!

Japanese

Kanpai

Pronunciation–Kan-pie!

Korean

Geonbae

Pronunciation–Gun-bae!

Portuguese

Saúde

Pronunciation–Saw-oo-de!

Russian

Будем здоровы/ На здоровье

Pronunciation–Budem zdorovi! / Na zdorovie!

Spanish

Salud

Pronunciation–Sah-lud!

Think of this scenario: You are sitting in a Tokyo restaurant. You just had the best sushi you have ever eaten. You get the bill, and then you think, "How much should I tip?" or "Is it customary to tip in restaurants in Japan?" How much to tip in a restaurant depends on the level of service and the country's tipping norm. In the US and Canada, it is common to tip between

15% and 20%. Canadian and US tourists might think that they should tip the same abroad, but this is often not the case. It is best to check in advance and follow the tipping customs in your traveling destination. Here are some tipping customs from around the world.

Waitstaff in Australia are paid living wages, so they aren't as reliant on tips as their US counterparts. Although tipping is not expected, it is fine to leave a tip if you enjoyed the service provided. In France, waitstaff make a meager wage in the restaurant industry. Usually, that is livable but not quite fancy. Sometimes you will find "service compris" on the bill, indicating that a surcharge has been added for service or that prices include an amount to compensate the staff. However, if a tip wasn't added to the bill, it is customary to leave up to 15% for good service. As for tipping in Mexico, there is a sliding scale of 10-15% based on the level of service provided. The same goes for the UK. Check the bill for an applied service fee—if there isn't one, use a sliding scale of 10-15%, depending on the level of service. In Italy, some venues such as restaurants, bars, and clubs may charge a cover charge (*pane e coperto*) and/or a service charge (*servizio*). Additional tipping is not expected, but it is common to round up the bill. In Spain, service fees are typically already added to the bill or into the pricing at most restaurants and bars. However, if it is a high-end establishment, an additional 10% tip is generally expected. When dining at a more casual establishment, a rounded-up tip is always appreciated but not expected. In Thailand, high-end restaurants often add a 10% service fee. If not, tipping 10% is customary. In more casual places, tipping is not expected but appreciated. If you wish to tip in Thailand, the easiest solution is to round up the bill's total.

There are countries where you shouldn't tip, for example, Japan. Tipping is not customary in Japan, as good service is always expected as a cultural norm. Tipping wasn't customary in China in the past, but it is becoming more popular, especially in tourist areas. Nowadays, some places add a service fee. But, there is no need to add a tip on top of the bill. In Hong Kong, many restaurants will add a 10%-15% service fee. There is no need to add a large tip on top of the bill, but rounding up the bill is common. In the UAE, 10%-15% is customary. 10% service charges are often added, so always check before leaving a tip. Portugal's tipping scheme is the most complicated on this list. 5% or bill roundup is customary in coffee shops and bars. 10% is customary in restaurants. However, always check for a service fee before tipping.

9

Driving a Car Abroad

Some people choose to rent a car while traveling abroad. It has its benefits—traveling without depending on public transportation—which can often be slow and limited in terms of where you can get with it. Before renting a car abroad, there are a few things to check. The first thing to check is what side of the road to drive. Most countries use the right-hand traffic (RHT) system where cars drive on the right side in bidirectional traffic. However, about a third of the world's population uses the left-hand traffic (LHT) system. Countries that use LHT include England, Japan, and Thailand. Many countries that use LHT are former parts of the British Empire and were influenced by its traffic rules. This includes India, Pakistan, South Africa, Australia, New Zealand, Hong Kong, Singapore, and some Caribbean islands like Jamaica, Antigua, and Barbuda.

Another thing to check before renting a car abroad is if your driver's license is valid or if you also need to have an International Driving Permit (IDP). IDP is a document that allows you to drive a motor vehicle in over 150 countries when it is accompanied by a valid driver's license. Some countries require drivers from abroad to possess an IDP. IDPs are not accepted by all countries, so it is essential to check before getting one. Rental car insurance is another crucial thing to check in advance. Insurance requirements differ between countries. Rental car insurance is often offered by the rental company. There are also third parties that provide rental car insurance. Some credit cards come with rental car insurance that is often limited.

Car rental age restrictions are also something to check. It is not surprising that there are minimum age requirements to rent a car abroad. However, in some countries, there are restrictions on renting a vehicle above a certain age. Take Ireland, for example. Some rental companies won't rent to drivers who are 80 or older. It is also common that those 75 and over are required to provide medical and insurance documents proving they are fit to drive and haven't had accidents in the past 5 years to rent a car.

There are also traffic rules that are unique to each country. You might find traffic rules that differ significantly from those in the place you live. For example, in Germany, drivers who run out of gas on the Autobahn, the German motorway, can be fined. This is because stopping on an Autobahn is not allowed. Running out of gas is considered a driver's error that can be avoided. German Autobahns are also famous for not having speed limits. However, there are speed limits in some areas. Another law from Germany is the ban on speed camera detectors. These detectors are a popular feature in navigation apps that can alert drivers of speed cameras. A similar ban also exists in France.

In some countries, car headlights should always be on while driving. Examples are Denmark, Switzerland, Sweden, and Bulgaria. In Japan, drivers can be fined for splashing pedestrians while driving through puddles. In Cyprus, it is illegal to eat or drink while driving, and in Thailand, it is unlawful to drive without a shirt on.

It is common to receive a driver's license after passing theory and practical tests where a driver demonstrates knowledge of traffic rules and the ability to follow them. However, in some countries, there are additional unique requirements. In Brazil, besides the theory and practical tests, drivers should pass a psychological evaluation to receive a driving license. Some Mexican jurisdictions require a driver's blood type to issue a driver's license. This information can be helpful in the event of an accident. Speaking of Mexico, not too long ago, there were no theory or practical driving tests to receive a driver's license in Mexico City. Mexico City residents could get a driver's license after providing documents, signing forms, and paying a fee. This was changed. Now drivers should pass theory and practical tests to get a license.

Some countries like Hungary, Denmark, and Switzerland require taking first-aid classes to get a driver's license. In 2013, The Sierra Leone Road Transport Authority (SLRTA) added a requirement for those who want to take a driver's test—to play a board game first. This game, "The Drivers' Way," teaches traffic laws. It was created by a police officer who wanted to make the learning of traffic laws more interesting. As with many fees, the cost of obtaining a driver's license varies between countries. In India, for example, it can be below US $7. While in Norway, the cost can reach US $3,675.

10

Unique Laws From Around the World

When traveling, it is crucial to check for laws in your destination before you travel. It can save you from unpleasant situations. Laws in your country may be similar to those in other places. However, there may also be unique laws that are worth knowing. Here are some rules from around the world.

The first country is Singapore, which is known for having unique laws. Singapore's first prime minister, Lee Kuan Yew, is considered the nation's founding father and is credited with turning Singapore into a developed country by striving toward perfection. Immaculate cleanliness is one area that represents their striving for perfection. Therefore, things that might be considered common sense in some places, like not littering or not spitting in public, are actual laws in Singapore. Other Singapore laws include a chewing-gum ban with some exceptions like for medical purposes, no graffiti, no jaywalking, and no connecting to strangers' Wi-Fi.

Canada also provides some interesting and unique laws. For example, in the eastern Canadian city of Halifax, limousine and taxi drivers should wear a shirt or a "military-type blouse" with sleeves and collar. And, they also need to wear shoes and socks with that shirt or "military-type blouse." Alberta's Occupational Health and Safety Code of 2009 mandates that a wooden ladder cannot be painted. The reason for this is to be able to tell the condition of the ladder. So if you are a professional wooden-ladder painter, don't look for a job in the province of Alberta. Another law that comes from Alberta is the ban on owning pet rats. Alberta is constantly working on being rat-free. There is also a hotline, 310-RATS (7287), which Albertans can call after spotting a rat. The last Canadian law in this list is that it is illegal to take a bandage off in public.

In Thailand, similar to Singapore, littering is illegal. Littering is wrong, no matter if it is legal or not. However, in Thailand, you can be fined for it. It is also illegal to leave your house without wearing underwear in Thailand. However, it isn't clear how this law is enforced. In Thailand, there is also a ban on e-cigarettes. This ban is not unique to Thailand. There are several countries where e-cigarette use is banned or restricted. In Mexico, for instance, there is a ban on importing vaping products. Another Mexican law is *Ley Seca*—Dry Law. It has been on the books in Mexico since 1915. The law is simple—no alcohol sales for at least 24 hours on or before election day. The reason is so voters will vote in a sober state. While it was formerly country-wide, it is now given to each state to enforce. Some may choose to enforce it only on election day, others on election day and the day before. And in some tourist areas, this law is not enforced at all.

Switzerland also has some unique laws. One of them is no standing and urinating after 10 PM, as Swiss law states the noise can disturb others. The same reasoning is behind a similar rule of not flushing the toilet after 10 PM. Homeowners can decide that these laws won't be enforced on their property if the mentioned actions don't cause disturbance for other people. In addition, Switzerland has set forth a law that no hiking may be done in the nude. This law was set after hikers were discovered doing precisely that, hiking in the nude in the conservative canton (region) of Appenzell. Finally, in Switzerland, there are a few things that you cannot do on Sunday. This includes mowing your lawn, hanging laundry to dry, or dropping your empty bottles and cans into the public recycling.

In Scottish courts, there are the typical "guilty" and "not guilty" verdicts, but there is also a third verdict of "not proven." In this case, the jury believes the plaintiff to be guilty but feels there is not enough evidence to prove their case. Following this third verdict, Scottish courtroom cases are considered "guilty until proven innocent." According to a South Australian law from 1992, if you intentionally disrupt a funeral service or wedding, you can find yourself receiving a $10,000 fine or imprisonment for 2 years. Another law that comes from South Australia is the ban on possessing 50 kgs (110 lb.) or more potatoes unless you are a member of the Potato Corporation or an authorized agent. The fine is $2,000 for your first offense or $5,000 for a subsequent violation.

Tourists should be careful when trying to take pictures of the impressive Buddhist temples of Sri Lanka. Some temples don't allow taking photos, while some do. If images are taken in a temple, they must be respectful. For example, a woman was deported for pretending to kiss a statue of Buddha. On a related note, having tattoos of Buddha can get you in trouble. A tourist was deported after authorities spotted a Buddha tattoo on her arm.

Taking photos or videos inside High-Security Zones (HSZs) is prohibited. HSZs include military sites, some government buildings, and official residences. HSZs aren't always marked. In the United Arab Emirates (UAE), it is also illegal to take photos of government buildings and military sites. UAE authorities take privacy very seriously. It is unlawful to take pictures of people without their consent. You could be facing a fine and even a jail sentence for posting an image of an individual without their permission.

Going either in or out of Morocco, there are limits to how much of the local currency (Moroccan Dirhams) a traveler can carry. In Morocco, there are also strict regulations around flying drones. Flying drones is prohibited unless there is permission from the Moroccan Civil Aviation Authority. Morocco is not alone. As drones became popular, some countries introduced restrictions on operating them. Reasons to restrict their use include security and protection of wildlife. Portugal has outlawed urinating in the ocean. However, it is not clear if anyone has been arrested for the crime. In 2009, Greece introduced regulations regarding what footwear visitors can wear when visiting historical sites. At sites like the Acropolis, wearing high heels is not allowed because they can damage the site.

In Japan, it is illegal to prepare *fugu* (blowfish) without a fugu-preparing license. Consuming fugu can be deadly, as the poison the fish generates is highly toxic and has killed many diners. Therefore, chefs undergo intense training for years before being given certificates proving their ability to handle the dangerous fish and prepare it safely. Speaking of fish, according to the Salmon Act of 1986 of the Parliament of the United Kingdom, you can be found guilty of "handling salmon in suspicious circumstances." Where "suspicious circumstances" means fished illegally according to other sections of the act.

In France, since the 1800s, you cannot name or address your pig as Napoleon. This law was passed during Napoleon's reign in France to prevent pranksters from making fun. At most public pools in France, no swimwear for men other than tight-fitting Speedo-type is allowed. This means no swimming trunks or board shorts. A French law from 1910 prohibits kissing by a train station platform while a train is on the platform. The law was introduced because of delays in train departures caused by couples kissing goodbye. Another French law is the ability to marry a dead person. This law was written into the books because of a national tragedy, the Malpasset Dam failure. Over 420 people lost their lives then. Irène Jodar's fiancé, André Capra was one of those poor souls. President at the time, Charles de Gaulle, signed the couple's marriage into reality even though the husband had passed already. Some criteria must be met to marry a deceased individual:

- There should be proof of clear intention of both parties to get married. Things like a purchase of a wedding dress or sent wedding invitations.
- The president of France must authorize the marriage.

Cycling is a popular way of transportation in Denmark, so there are several rules around riding a bike. One of them is the prohibition on riding while drunk. Riding a bike while intoxicated can land you a fine of 1,500 DKK, which's around $240 US. While Denmark doesn't have a BAC (Blood Alcohol Content) guideline for cyclists, you will be fined if the police believe that your biking poses a danger to you or others. Another Danish law specifies what name parents can choose for their baby. The Danish government carries a list of approved baby names. If parents want to use a name that is not on the list, they should get government approval.

The laws and regulations above provide little detail. They are meant to illustrate that laws can be unpredictable. The list above might change and be inaccurate when you travel. You need to check before you travel for laws in your destination.

11

Funny Travel Stories

If you like to travel, you for sure have funny stories—translation misunderstandings—not knowing local customs, etc. Here are a few funny travel stories.

Don't Rock the Boat

The first one is about a family who decided to rent a pontoon boat and spend the day on a Florida sandbar. When it was time to return, they got back onto the pontoon and began sailing back. As the family was making its way back, the boat started to slow down progressively. Fearing the worst, the family members paused to restart the engine, but then the bow began to sink into the water, with the engine rising out of the water at the back. They dashed to the back, trying to even the load, but it wasn't working. Panicking, they began bailing out the boat with Dixie cups, hoping to clear out enough water to stay afloat. It was only after the engine went high enough in the air that they noticed there was no anchor at the front of the boat—it had fallen off. They had been unknowingly dragging it until it stuck and caused a panic.

Halloween Is in My Blood

The next story is from an American student studying abroad. When studying in Vienna, Austria, during college, the student decided to get dressed up for Halloween, just as he and his friends would have in the United States. However, as he lived far from downtown, he had to use public transportation to get to his friend's place. At some point, he realized, looking around, that nobody else was dressed up. He quickly learned that Austrians don't dress up for Halloween and that someone in fake blood and makeup will scare everyone by taking public transportation when they're the only one wearing a costume.

There Is Nothing Like a Relaxing Shower

A tourist was lucky enough to stay in a luxury hotel during his visit to the USA. However, not sure he would be welcomed back after the events of this story. He was trying to take a quick shower on the morning of the checkout. He stepped in and turned the knob to start the water, but no water. Then he turned it again, nothing still. He continued turning the knob until it finally came off the wall. At that instant, a gush of water started shooting out. He desperately tried to put the knob back but couldn't replace it. Water was shooting out so fast that the bathtub was filling up. He was now ankle deep. He jumped out, grabbed a towel, and ran out into the hallway for help. The first thing he spotted was a maid's cart. He ran up, but the woman did not speak English, so he simply grabbed her by the hand and ran her to his room. The instant she saw, she ran out to get help. Managers ran around left and right into the room and back out, trying to find someone who knew how to shut the water off while he stood there with only a towel on. Another maid came in and offered to let him into another room to finish his shower, along with complimentary breakfast, but he waved them off. He had a flight to catch.

Sweet Dreams

A traveler had been stranded in the airport for 24 hours and finally got her flight from Moscow to Copenhagen. Once she settled into her seat, she fell asleep right away. When she woke up, she was startled to realize that she couldn't lift her feet. In a panic, she looked down, only to see that the woman ahead of her was transporting honey. The jar had spilled and had glued her feet to the floor. The woman in front was asleep and had no clue.

I Have Not Slept Gun Wink

Nowadays, services such as Airbnb are pretty popular. Tourists can stay at privately owned properties rather than hotels. Here is a funny story about a gentleman who rented out his basement. This older gentleman likes to mess around with the latest tech. He bought two electronic locks, putting one on the basement door leading to the Airbnb room and the other on his front door. For some reason, he put the same code on both. One night, two young female tourists came to stay in the room. However, they weren't paying attention and came the wrong way through the front door. The old man woke up hearing the commotion in his house, got out of bed, grabbed his shotgun, and ran downstairs in his underwear. Of course, the girls saw him, started screaming, and ran out into the street. They continued screaming as they ran down the street, waking up the entire neighborhood. At some point, the mistake was figured out, and the girls were shown to their real Airbnb. Somehow, the girls found the whole situation funny. They even left him with a five-star review after their stay.

AirB&Screem

A family of four got an Airbnb in the historic part of Cartagena, Colombia—a tiny condo with a kitchen, sleeping loft, and a living room. Little did they know that the condo's owner owned a tattoo parlor on the other side of the wall. Throughout their entire stay, they were jolted by the wails of customers being inked. On the positive side, they learned some Spanish curse words.

Long D'Eh

On a long road trip to Canada, a family stopped at the border crossing to enter. The border patrol guard asked the father a routine question: "Sir, can you name the children in the car with you?" Then, so tired he could barely see straight, he couldn't do it. They took him in for questioning.

The More the Marry-Er

A lucky bride, her husband's parents gifted them a week at an all-inclusive hotel resort for their honeymoon. However, things quickly turned sour. The happy couple realized that the groom's parents had also booked a room on-site for the week and wanted nothing more than an entire week of group activities. The troubled couple even faked not feeling well to try and avoid an all-family dinner. "They just got room service to our room and sat with us while we faked stomach aches. Outside of this, we see them maybe 2 or 3 times a year for a couple of days at a time as he finds them a bit overbearing at times, and they don't really like me," the bride wrote in her desperate post. The groom's parents would arrive at 6 AM every morning, knocking on the door and getting them up for breakfast to prepare for another day of group activities. The couple eventually did get fed up and addressed their need for "alone time." The groom's parents shrugged them off, explaining, "that's what the room is for."

The unhappy bride took it to Reddit, asking users if they would be in the wrong for using their saved-up honeymoon money to leave the hotel and head out for another town they wanted to visit, leaving the parents behind. The bride clarified in her post: "We could also book a few days in a nice hotel for about half of what's left in our wedding/honeymoon fund." She wrote, adding that they could "use the remainder of the week we booked off in another town without his parents knowing we'd left until we had." In good news, the bride wrote a follow-up sharing that they had indeed booked a hotel for four days in the town they wanted to visit. She wrote from a train, putting in her post, "Should be arriving in our final station in the next 30 minutes." So, what can we learn from this story? Next time you book a vacation in an all-inclusive hotel, make sure it doesn't **include** your partner's parents.

GoPro Yourself

An Irish man borrowed his son's GoPro for a first-time Las Vegas visit, using a selfie stick to help take the footage. However, poor dad didn't quite understand how to use the device and instead only caught footage of himself for the duration of the trip, as the GoPro was pointed backward. The son has posted his dad's footage on YouTube, where it has been watched by millions of sympathetic (but still laughing) people.

This Is My Seat

When a man boarded his flight from London to Galway, he didn't know what, or more like, who would be awaiting him. As he reached his seat, he realized that he was already sitting there. How is it possible, you ask? The man sitting in the seat was an exact look-alike to the man. The two men took a moment to take a photo together, which became viral. To make the story even stranger, they stayed in the same hotel at their destination. They even ran into each other at a pub.

Joyride

One traveler reported on their admittedly unusual experience traveling from Lake Wenchi to Addis Ababa in Ethiopia by bus. "I had not only the bumpiest journey of my life but also the most bizarre. Chickens casually strolling around nibbling on my toes, two goats strapped on the roof, people sitting on my lap meanwhile the driver also acted as a DJ playing only ABBA tunes for 3 hours. Loved it."

12

Trivia Questions

1) What airports do the following codes represent?
PEK, LHR, CDG, DEL, LAS, MEX, EWR, SYD, YYZ, SEA

2) What are the capital cities of the following countries:

Part 1:
England, South Korea, Japan, Portugal, Norway, Argentina, Egypt, Ukraine, Bulgaria, Romania, Pakistan, Bahrain, Colombia, Ethiopia, Sri Lanka, Taiwan

Part 2 (tricky):
Switzerland, Brazil, Canada, New Zealand, Turkey, Morocco, South Africa, Bolivia, Australia

3) What are the 50 US states?

4) Are you familiar with the following geographical syndromes?

- Florence

- Paris
- Jerusalem
- India

5) What are the 10 largest countries by population?

6) What currencies are used in the following countries?
Afghanistan, Argentina, Brazil, China, Cyprus, Egypt, Ethiopia, India, Iran, Israel, Japan, South Korea, Philippines, Russia, Turkey

7) What are the 10 largest countries by area?

13

Trivia Answers

1) Airport codes

IATA Code	Airport	Location	Country
PEK	Beijing Capital International Airport	Chaoyang-Shunyi, Beijing	China
LHR	Heathrow Airport	Hillingdon, London	United Kingdom
CDG	Charles de Gaulle Airport	Roissy-en-France, Île-de-France	France
DEL	Indira Gandhi International Airport	New Delhi	India
LAS	McCarran International Airport	Las Vegas, Nevada	United States
MEX	Benito Juárez International Airport	Venustiano Carranza, Mexico City	Mexico
EWR	Newark Liberty International Airport	Newark, New Jersey	United States
SYD	Sydney Kingsford-Smith Airport	Mascot, New South Wales	Australia
YYZ	Toronto Pearson International Airport	Mississauga, Ontario	Canada
SEA	Seattle–Tacoma International Airport	SeaTac, Washington	United States

2) Capital cities

Part 1:

England → London

South Korea → Seoul

Japan → Tokyo

Portugal → Lisbon

Norway → Oslo
Argentina → Buenos Aires
Egypt → Cairo
Ukraine → Kiev
Bulgaria → Sofia
Romania → Bucharest
Pakistan → Islamabad
Bahrain → Manama
Colombia → Bogotá
Ethiopia → Addis Ababa
Sri Lanka → Colombo
Taiwan → Taipei

Part 2 (tricky):

Switzerland → Bern

Today, 26 cantons (like states) make up Switzerland. In the past, cantons operated as their own sovereign states. Then, in 1848, the Swiss federal state was created, uniting all cantons together into one state. Today, each canton possesses its own capital, government, and constitution but is maintained by the federal state, and Bern serves as the main capital.

Brazil → Brasilia

In 1960, Brasilia was founded as Brazil's new capital. It was constructed as the testing ground for a city of the future, placed in a more central location than Rio de Janeiro, which had been the capital up until then. Architect Oscar Niemeyer and urbanist Lucio Costa designed the city.

Canada → Ottawa

The capital "title" jumped around Canada between 1841 and 1866. Kingston, Montreal, Toronto, and Quebec City were all the capitals of the Province of Canada. Finally, in 1857, Queen Victoria chose Ottawa as the capital. It became the functional legislative capital in 1866 and was officially made the capital of the Dominion of Canada with Confederation in 1867 and has stayed the capital ever since.

New Zealand → Wellington

Auckland is commonly mistaken as New Zealand's capital as it has the highest population. However, in fact, Wellington has been the capital since 1865.

Turkey → Ankara

Istanbul is the largest city in Turkey. However, it is not the capital. The second-largest city, Ankara, is the capital of Turkey. It has been the capital since the independence declaration in 1923. Ankara enjoys a rich history influenced by Greek, Persian, Roman, Byzantine, and Ottoman civilizations. These influences can be seen in various archeological sites.

Morocco → Rabat

Rabat serves as the capital of Morocco even though many tend to believe Marrakech or Casablanca to be the capital, thanks to their popularity.

South Africa → Cape Town, Pretoria, and Bloemfontein

South Africa doesn't have a single capital city where all branches of government reside. Instead, its three branches of government are split over different cities: legislative Cape Town, executive Pretoria, and judicial Bloemfontein.

Australia → Canberra

Until 1927, Melbourne operated as Australia's capital, but that year the government moved to Canberra, where the capital still resides today. This was a work in process, as Sydney and Melbourne fought for the title of capital years before—the two cities came to a compromise, agreeing to design Canberra to become the capital.

3) US states

(Hint) numbers on the right specify how many state names start with the letters on the left:

A → 4
C → 3
D → 1
F → 1
G → 1
H → 1
I → 4
K → 2
L → 1
M → 8
N → 8
O → 3
P → 1
R → 1
S → 2
T → 2
U → 1
V → 2
W → 4

Answer:

Alabama	Louisiana	Ohio
Alaska	Maine	Oklahoma
Arizona	Maryland	Oregon
Arkansas	Massachusetts	Pennsylvania
California	Michigan	Rhode Island
Colorado	Minnesota	South Carolina
Connecticut	Mississippi	South Dakota
Delaware	Missouri	Tennessee
Florida	Montana	Texas
Georgia	Nebraska	Utah
Hawaii	Nevada	Vermont
Idaho	New Hampshire	Virginia
Illinois	New Jersey	Washington
Indiana	New Mexico	West Virginia
Iowa	New York	Wisconsin
Kansas	North Carolina	Wyoming
Kentucky	North Dakota	

4) Geographical syndromes

Certain locations have an indelible effect on the lives of their visitors, but what about their physical or mental health as well? A few cities in this wide world are known to have extreme effects on their visitors.

Florence (Stendhal) Syndrome

Stendhal syndrome, also known as Florence syndrome, can cause rapid heartbeat, fainting, confusion, and hallucinations.

It is known to strike individuals who are exposed to objects or phenomena of intense beauty. 19th-century French author Stendhal wrote the first account of the Stendhal syndrome, after whom it is named, in his 1817 visit to Florence in his book *Naples and Florence: A Journey from Milan to Reggio.*

Stendhal wrote:

"I was in a sort of ecstasy, from the idea of being in Florence, close to the great men whose tombs I had seen. Absorbed in the contemplation of sublime beauty... I reached the point where one encounters celestial sensations... everything spoke so vividly to my soul. Ah, if I could only forget. I had palpitations of the heart, what in Berlin they call 'nerves'. Life was drained from me. I walked with the fear of falling."

Florence art has caused numerous cases of people fainting or feeling dizzy and requiring medical attention over the years. For example, in 2018, the Uffizi Gallery in Florence was host to a tourist who had a heart attack while admiring Sandro Botticelli's The Birth of Venus.

Paris Syndrome

The Paris syndrome is a feeling of disappointment displayed by some individuals when visiting Paris, France. Sometimes, this disappointment can cause symptoms like anxiety and hallucinations. Although this syndrome was witnessed in tourists from different countries, it has been particularly observed in Japanese tourists.

In 2004, the president of the Franco-Japanese Medical Association hypothesized that the media is to blame for the existence of the syndrome. He claimed that popular media's hyper-attractive description of France, Paris in particular, causes episodes as tourists are quickly slapped into the reality that the streets are not teeming with models and cigar-smoking gents sipping wine. Instead, the city is very much like any other—there are homeless populations, trash, and traffic jams.

There is no doubt that Paris is a great travel destination. It has beautiful architecture, fine dining, high-end clothing, and world-class museums. However, people visiting Paris should have realistic expectations and keep in mind that, like other cities, it also has its imperfections.

Jerusalem and India Syndromes

Judaism, Christianity, and Islam all consider Jerusalem to be a holy city. Some people who visit Jerusalem experience religiously themed obsessive ideas, delusions, or other psychosis-like experiences often referred to as "Jerusalem syndrome." Examples of the Jerusalem syndrome are tourists who claim to be the Messiah. Some with the syndrome have a history of psychiatric illness, while others don't. Reported cases document that the mental condition usually improves and passes within a few weeks or when the individual is removed from Jerusalem. India syndrome is a spirituality-related phenomenon, just like the Jerusalem syndrome. In India syndrome, westerners who visit India exhibit delusional behavior following spiritual practices such as meditation, yoga, and visiting sacred sites.

5) 10 largest countries by population (2021 estimates)

China → 1,439,323,776

India → 1,380,004,385

United States → 331,002,651
Indonesia → 273,523,615
Pakistan → 220,892,340
Brazil → 212,559,417
Nigeria → 206,139,589
Bangladesh → 164,689,383
Russia → 145,934,462
Mexico → 128,932,753

6) Currencies used in different countries
Afghanistan → Afghan afghani
Argentina → Argentine peso
Brazil → Brazilian real
China → Chinese yuan
Cyprus → Euro
Egypt → Egyptian pound
Ethiopia → Ethiopian birr
India → Indian rupee
Iran → Iranian rial
Israel → Israeli new shekel
Japan → Japanese yen
South Korea → South Korean won
Philippines → Philippine peso
Russia → Russian ruble
Turkey → Turkish lira

7) 10 largest countries by area (in descending order)
Russia
Canada
China
United States

Brazil
Australia
India
Argentina
Kazakhstan
Algeria

References

1. Xim. (2018, October 2). *Airlines verifying your credit card at check-in*. Triptipedia. https://www.triptipedia.com/tip/dg6si2W/airlines-verifying-your-credit-card-at-check-in
2. Ocampo, J. (2020, February 10). *Do you need the credit card you used to book a flight to check in?* Lifehacker. https://lifehacker.com/do-you-need-the-credit-card-you-used-to-book-a-flight-t-1841518910
3. Skip. (n.d.). *6 month validity passport guide: What you need to know*. https://helloskip.com/blog/6-month-validity-passport-guide-what-you-need-to-know/?ref=YGPages
4. Brumelis, O. (2020, May 21). *What information to write on luggage tags (guide)*. Clever Journey. https://www.cleverjourney.com/luggage-tags-guide
5. Rayburn-Trobaug C. (2018, July 31). *What not to put on luggage tags*. Travel Tips - USA Today. https://traveltips.usatoday.com/not-put-luggage-tags-13407.html
6. Mental Floss. (2015, May 18). *10 smart things to pack in your carry-on (And one not to)*. https://www.mentalfloss.com/article/63899/10-smart-things-pack-your-carry-and-one-not
7. Teel, C. M. (2021, March 30). *Which U.S. airlines are most likely to lose your luggage?* Airfarewatchdog. https://www

.airfarewatchdog.com/blog/44256814/the-u-s-airlines-most-likely-to-lose-your-luggage

8. IATA. (n.d.). *Airline and location code search.* https://www.iata.org/en/publications/directories/code-search
9. Wikipedia. (2002, November 23). *IATA airport code.* Retrieved July 1, 2021, from https://en.wikipedia.org/wiki/IATA_airport_code
10. Crockett, Z. (2020, June 30). *Why is airport food so expensive?* The Hustle. https://thehustle.co/airport-food-expensive
11. Airports Council International. (n.d.). *America's airports: Did you know?* https://airportsforthefuture.org/did-you-know
12. Hardiman, J. (2021, June 26). *How do airports actually make money?* Simple Flying. https://simpleflying.com/how-airports-make-money
13. Mental Floss. (2015, March 15). *15 incredible behind-the-scenes airport facts.* https://www.mentalfloss.com/article/62172/15-incredible-behind-scenes-airport-facts
14. Singh, S. (2019, November 5). *Could capsule hotels in airports reinvent long layovers?* Simple Flying. https://simpleflying.com/airport-capsule-hotels
15. Ho, E. (2021, March 22). *These are the airports that offer winter coat checks.* Map Happy. https://maphappy.org/2015/11/dude-you-can-leave-the-winter-coat-at-the-airport
16. Aero Corner. (2020, July 2). *Do (Commercial) airplanes & helicopters have keys to start?* https://aerocorner.com/blog/do-airplanes-have-keys
17. BAA Training. (2019, February 26). *Top 10 interesting facts about aviation.* https://www.baatraining.com/top-10-interesting-facts-about-aviation

18. Crow, S. (2019, July 11). *45 amazing airplane facts that will make your mind soar*. Best Life. https://bestlifeonline.com/airplane-facts
19. Moskvitch, K. (2015, January 12). *Why does food taste different on planes?* BBC. https://www.bbc.com/future/article/20150112-why-in-flight-food-tastes-weird
20. Gizauskas, R. (2018, January 26). *There is actually a way to legally drink your own booze on flights*. The Sun. https://www.thesun.co.uk/travel/5422561/how-to-drink-own-alcohol-on-flight
21. Nast, C. (2019, February 21). *Do babies born on airplanes get visa-free travel across the world?* Condé Nast Traveller-India. https://www.cntraveller.in/story/explained-happens-baby-born-airplane/#s-custglendullan-distillery
22. Wikipedia. (2005, September 8). *Blue ice (aviation)*. https://en.wikipedia.org/wiki/Blue_ice_(aviation)
23. Manneh, E. (2020, February 12). *What actually happens when you flush an airplane toilet?* Reader's Digest. https://www.rd.com/article/flush-airplane-toilet
24. Cahn, L. (2020, March 9). *20 common myths about airplanes you need to stop believing*. Reader's Digest. https://www.rd.com/list/airplane-myths
25. Harris, T. (n.d.). *How airline crews work*. HowStuffWorks. https://science.howstuffworks.com/transport/flight/modern/airline-crew1.htm
26. Claiborne, M. (2020, August 8). *Do private Jets need two pilots?* Aero Corner. https://www.aircraftcompare.com/blog/do-jets-need-two-pilots
27. Hoeller, S. (2015, August 3). *See the secret airplane bedrooms where flight attendants sleep on long-haul flights*. Business Insider. https://www.businessinsider.com/secret-airpla

ne-bedrooms-2015-7

28. Bywater, T., & Godfrey, K. G. (2019, April 10). *Hidden plane features you didn't know about including horns & pedals.* The Sun. https://www.thesun.co.uk/travel/7450088/planes-secret-buttons-hidden-features
29. De Graaf, J. (2019, February 14). *Does a plane have a horn?* KLM Blog. https://blog.klm.com/does-a-plane-have-a-horn/
30. McCartney, S. (2018, February 14). *How much of your $355 ticket is profit for airlines?* WSJ. https://www.wsj.com/articles/how-much-of-your-355-ticket-is-profit-for-airlines-1518618600
31. Smith, L. (2017, March 16). *How do airlines make their money? Hint – it's not by selling economy seats.* International Business Times UK. https://www.ibtimes.co.uk/how-do-airlines-make-their-money-hint-its-not-by-selling-economy-seats-1612010
32. Hoeller, S. (2018, November 21). *Flight attendants reveal the first things they notice when travelers board a plane.* Insider. https://www.insider.com/what-flight-attendants-look-for-when-boarding-2017-3
33. Sims, M. (2020, October 15). *Flight attendants reveal 14 things they wish all passengers would start doing.* Insider. https://www.insider.com/how-to-make-flight-attendants-like-you-2020-1
34. Wikipedia. (2006, July 9). *Aircraft seat map.* https://en.wikipedia.org/wiki/Aircraft_seat_map
35. Sutherland-Miller, J. (2019, November 9). *A (Painfully) honest guide to airplane etiquette.* Tortuga. https://blog.tortugabackpacks.com/airplane-etiquette/
36. Crislip, K. (2019, June 26). *Follow these airplane etiquette*

rules for a happy flight. TripSavvy. https://www.tripsavvy.com/airplane-etiquette-rules-for-a-happy-flight-3150253

37. Morin, A. (2016, April 28). *Talking to the stranger next to you on a plane makes you happy, according to science.* Inc. https://www.inc.com/amy-morin/talking-to-the-stranger-next-to-you-on-a-plane-makes-you-happy-according-to-scie.html
38. Sampson, H. (2019, September 19). *How did clapping on planes become such a divisive issue?* The Washington Post. https://www.washingtonpost.com/travel/2019/09/19/how-did-clapping-planes-become-such-divisive-issue
39. Condé Nast Traveler. (2016, April 7). *Please don't clap when the plane lands.* https://www.cntraveler.com/stories/2016-04-07/please-dont-clap-when-the-plane-lands
40. Cox, J. (2019, October 31). *Ask the captain: Do pilots like it when passengers clap after landing?* USA TODAY. https://www.usatoday.com/story/travel/columnist/cox/2019/10/31/ask-captain-what-do-pilots-think-post-landing-applause/2502515001
41. Royce, H. (2018, August 9). *Here's why you should never clap when a plane lands.* Now To Love. https://www.nowtolove.com.au/travel/travel-news/heres-why-you-should-never-clap-when-a-plane-lands-39485
42. SmarterTravel. (2019, October 3). *How to avoid jet lag: Prevention and remedies.* https://www.smartertravel.com/avoid-jet-lag-prevention-remedies
43. Ellwood, M. (2017, July 21). *Why you should never eat food on planes, and other jet-set tips.* NationalPost. https://nationalpost.com/travel/why-you-should-never-eat-food-on-planes-and-other-jet-set-tips

44. Lakritz, T. (2020, March 10). *12 of the longest flight routes in the world.* Insider. https://www.insider.com/longest-flight-routes-in-the-world
45. American Airlines. (n.d.) https://www.aa.com
46. Wikipedia. (2007, April 13). *First class (aviation).* https://en.wikipedia.org/wiki/First_class_(aviation)
47. Sampson, H. (2019, November 15). *Airline classes are important. Here's how to know which one you need.* The Washington Post. https://www.washingtonpost.com/travel/2019/11/15/airline-fares-are-complicated-heres-how-know-which-one-you-need
48. Retrowow. (n.d.). *History of business class flights.* https://www.retrowow.co.uk/transport/air_travel/business_class.html
49. Wikipedia. (2008, May 30). *Business class airline.* https://en.wikipedia.org/wiki/Business_class_airline
50. Myers, D. (2015, November 25). *How is airplane food warmed up during a flight?* The Daily Meal. https://www.thedailymeal.com/eat/how-airplane-food-warmed-during-flight
51. Krans, B. (2019, October 14). *Flight attendants avoid drinking tap water on planes, you should too.* Healthline. https://www.healthline.com/health-news/how-safe-is-the-water-coffee-tea-on-your-favorite-airline#Ranking-airline-water-quality
52. Puckett, J. (2019, September 30). *Study shows airplane water is dirtier than you think.* Condé Nast Traveler. https://www.cntraveler.com/story/study-shows-airplane-water-is-dirtier-than-you-think
53. Wei, W. (2017, December 13). *Why airplane Windows have tiny holes.* Business Insider. https://www.businessinsider.

com/airplane-windows-tiny-holes-2016-3

54. Wei, W. (2017, May 19). *Here's how many planes are in the air at any moment.* Travel + Leisure. https://www.travelandleisure.com/airlines-airports/number-of-planes-in-air
55. Asquith, J. (2021, June 29). *Do you know what the world's busiest flight route is with 180 daily flights?* Forbes. https://www.forbes.com/sites/jamesasquith/2020/01/21/do-you-know-what-the-worlds-busiest-flight-route-is-with-180-daily-flights/#2273c773702e
56. Schrader, R. (2019, September 16). *20 shocking facts about air travel.* TripSavvy. https://www.tripsavvy.com/shocking-facts-about-air-travel-3498983
57. Hacobian, C. (2018, June 27). *Here's how high planes actually fly, according to experts.* Time. https://time.com/5309905/how-high-do-planes-fly
58. Aero Corner. (2021, May 4). *How fast do airplanes go? (during takeoff, flight, landing).* https://www.aircraftcompare.com/blog/how-fast-do-airplanes-go
59. Statista. (2021, April 30). *Airline industry worldwide - number of flights 2004-2021.* https://www.statista.com/statistics/564769/airline-industry-number-of-flights
60. Debczak, M. (2017, June 30). *Why certain airplane seats have a triangle above them.* Mental Floss. https://www.mentalfloss.com/article/502437/why-certain-airplane-seats-have-triangle-above-them
61. Licea, M. (2019, July 29). *World's most frequent flyer has an insane weekly itinerary.* New York Post. https://nypost.com/2019/07/27/worlds-most-frequent-flyer-has-an-insane-weekly-itinerary
62. Finlay, M. (2020, September 8). *Why most aircraft are*

painted white. Simple Flying. https://simpleflying.com/why-most-aircraft-are-painted-white

63. Aero Corner. (2020, July 27). *Why most airplanes are painted white (And the exception).* https://aerocorner.com/blog/why-are-airplanes-white/
64. Bolluyt, J. (2018, August 10). *How much do flight attendants make?* Showbiz Cheat Sheet. https://www.cheatsheet.com/culture/how-much-do-flight-attendants-make.html
65. Simple Flying. (n.d.). *How many days does a flight attendant work in a month?* https://simpleflying.com/how-many-days-does-a-flight-attendant-work-in-a-month
66. Bakx, K. (2014, October 2). *Flight attendants claim WestJet often breaks minimum wage standards | CBC news.* CBC. https://www.cbc.ca/news/business/westjet-minimum-wage-cupe-cfau-1.4575681
67. Calfas, J. (2018, February 14). *Here's how much flight attendants make.* Money. https://money.com/how-much-do-flight-attendants-make/
68. Pardes, A., & Santilli, M. (2020, July 2). *Flight attendants share what it's really like to do their job right now.* Cosmopolitan. https://www.cosmopolitan.com/career/a52657/flight-attendant-things-i-wish-i-knew
69. Gillett, R. (2017, November 17). *Here's what it's REALLY like to be a Delta Air Lines flight attendant, one of the most competitive jobs out there.* Business Insider. https://www.businessinsider.com/heres-what-its-really-like-to-be-a-flight-attendant-2015-9#choosing-where-to-fly-8
70. LIVE JAPAN. (2019, September 26). *5 essential chopstick etiquette tips to know in Japan!* https://livejapan.com/en/in-tokyo/in-pref-tokyo/in-tokyo_train_station/article-a0001284

71. Putinja, I. (2017, September 12). *12 things you should never do in Japan*. Business Insider. https://www.businessinsider.com/12-things-you-should-never-do-in-japan-2017-9
72. Boyd, M. (2013, June 5). *How to be polite when eating at a Japanese restaurant*. Food & Nutrition Magazine. https://foodandnutrition.org/blogs/stone-soup/polite-eating-japanese-restaurant
73. Japan-Guide. (2021, February 27). *Japanese table manners*. https://www.japan-guide.com/e/e2005.html
74. Travel + Leisure. (n.d.). *20 amazing things you should never do in other countries*. https://travleisure.com/20-amazing-things-you-should-never-do-in-other-countries
75. Cichanowicz, L. (2016, May 9). *11 surprising customs from around the world*. Culture Trip. https://theculturetrip.com/north-america/usa/articles/12-surprising-customs-from-around-the-world
76. Racoma, B. (2019, August 29). *20 fascinating cultural traditions around the world*. Day Translations Blog. https://www.daytranslations.com/blog/20-traditions-around-the-world
77. Pittore, R. (2018, September 10). *Strange cultural traditions around the world*. AllTheRooms - The Vacation Rental Experts. https://www.alltherooms.com/blog/dark-tourism-the-most-unusual-customs-around-the-world
78. Sood, S. (2012, November 29). *The origins of bathhouse culture around the world*. BBC. https://www.bbc.com/travel/story/20121129-the-origins-of-bathhouse-culture-around-the-world
79. Palzer, K. (n.d.). *Banya - the Russian way to enjoy a sauna*. Deutsche Welle. https://www.dw.com/en/banya-the-rus

sian-way-to-enjoy-a-sauna/a-19008849

80. Learn Russian Language. (2019, July 16). *7 differences between Russian Banya and sauna.* https://learnrussianlanguage.net/differences-between-russian-banya-and-sauna
81. Wikipedia. (2021, June 13). *Onsen.* Retrieved July 7, 2021, from https://en.wikipedia.org/wiki/Onsen
82. Wikipedia. (2006, September 23). *Jjimjilbang.* Retrieved July 7, 2021, from https://en.wikipedia.org/wiki/Jjimjilbang
83. Mattia, N., & Park, A. (2020, November 6). *45 fascinating wedding traditions from around the world.* Brides. https://www.brides.com/gallery/wedding-traditions-around-the-world
84. Wikipedia. (2010, February 19). *Marriage and wedding customs in the Philippines.* https://en.wikipedia.org/wiki/Marriage_and_wedding_customs_in_the_Philippines
85. Wikipedia. (2006, May 15). *Money dance.* https://en.wikipedia.org/wiki/Money_dance
86. HuffPost. (2017, December 7). *The art of birth.* https://www.huffpost.com/entry/world-birthing-traditions_n_7033790
87. Bali Spirit. (n.d.). *Ceremonies.* https://www.balispirit.com/community/ceremony-family
88. Schalken, L. (2005, October 3). *Birth customs around the world.* Parents. https://www.parents.com/pregnancy/giving-birth/vaginal/birth-customs-around-the-world
89. Locker, M. (2016, December 21). *How to tip in 25 countries around the world.* Travel + Leisure. https://www.travelandleisure.com/travel-tips/budgeting-currency/global-tipping-etiquette

90. Travel Channel. (2018, May 27). *How to tip around the world.* https://www.travelchannel.com/interests/food-and-drink/photos/how-to-tip-around-the-world
91. Wikipedia. (2003, April 20). *Left and right-hand traffic.* https://en.wikipedia.org/wiki/Left-_and_right-hand_traffic
92. Rhino Car Hire. (n.d.). *Drive left or right - Which countries drive on the left or right.* https://www.rhinocarhire.com/Drive-Smart-Blog/Drive-Left-or-Right.aspx
93. Driving Tests. (2018, March 14). *International driver's license (Permit): Six things to know.* https://driving-tests.org/beginner-drivers/international-drivers-license
94. Perkins, E. (2020, March 11). *9 nasty truths of car rental insurance you need to know.* SmarterTravel. https://www.smartertravel.com/car-rental-insurance
95. Car Rental Ireland. (n.d.). *Car rental Ireland.* https://www.carrentalireland.com/age-restrictions.php
96. Auto Europe. (2021, May 10). https://www.autoeurope.com
97. *The world's 9 most unusual rules involving cars.* (2020, June 5). SIXT. https://www.sixt.com/magazine/travel/unusual-driving-rules
98. Wikipedia. (2005, April 19). *Autobahn.* https://en.wikipedia.org/wiki/Autobahn
99. SmarterTravel. (2014, April 27). *10 crazy driving laws around the world.* HuffPost. https://www.huffpost.com/entry/10-crazy-driving-laws-aro_b_4853354
100. Guided Motorbike Tours Ltd. (2020, 5). *Germany ban speed camera detectors.* https://www.guidedmotorbiketours.co.uk/germany-ban-speed-camera-detectors
101. ThaiResidents. (2018, May 23). *5 weird laws you are subject*

to in Thailand. https://thairesidents.com/lifestyle/5-weird-laws-subject-thailand

102. Olito, F. (2018, October 31). *Here's what it takes to get a driver's license in 13 countries around the world.* Insider. https://www.insider.com/drivers-license-around-world-2018-10
103. Wikipedia. (2009, April 12). *Driving licence in Brazil.* https://en.wikipedia.org/wiki/Driving_licence_in_Brazil
104. Angloinfo. (n.d.). *Mexican driving licenses.* https://www.angloinfo.com/how-to/mexico/transport/driving-licenses/driving-test
105. Mexico News Daily. (2017, January 7). *Driver exams will be mandatory in Mexico City next year.* https://mexiconewsdaily.com/news/drivers-will-be-tested-in-cdmx-next-year
106. HealthFirst. (2019, December 13). *Swiss drivers' license first aid course with accreditation.* https://www.healthfirst.ch/public-courses/first-aid-course-for-the-swiss-drivers-licence
107. Deutsche Welle. (n.d.). *Board game to improve road safety in Sierra Leone.* https://www.dw.com/en/board-game-to-improve-road-safety-in-sierra-leone/a-17305255
108. Slauer, S. (2018, October 5). *Here's how much it costs to get a driver's license in 20 different countries around the world.* Insider. https://www.insider.com/countries-cost-price-driver-license-comparison-2018-9
109. Jones, S. (2021, April 26). *Driving licence and learning licence fees in India.* Cars24. https://www.cars24.com/blog/driving-licence-fees
110. Wikipedia. (2002, July 27). *Lee Kuan yew.* https://en.wikip

edia.org/wiki/Lee_Kuan_Yew

111. Metz, E. (2015, March 28). *Why Singapore banned chewing gum.* BBC News. https://www.bbc.com/news/magazine-32090420
112. Avakian, T. (2015, August 4). *16 odd things that are illegal in Singapore.* Business Insider. https://www.businessinsider.com/things-that-are-illegal-in-singapore-2015-7
113. Simpson, H. (2017, June 21). *11 ways you'll get arrested in Canada.* Culture Trip. https://theculturetrip.com/north-america/canada/articles/11-ways-youll-get-arrested-in-canada
114. Donnell Law Group. (2017, August 6). *Strange laws in Canada.* https://www.donnellgroup.ca/b/some-of-the-strangest-laws-in-canada.html
115. Tucker, E. (2015, March 11). *Don't paint a wooden ladder in Alberta & 11 more quirky Canadian laws.* Global News. https://globalnews.ca/news/1877371/dont-paint-a-wooden-ladder-in-alberta-11-more-quirky-canadian-laws
116. The Canadian Press. (2015, January 20). *Spot a rat? Alberta sets up hotline to rat out rodents.* https://www.cbc.ca/news/canada/edmonton/rat-hotline-encourages-rodent-reporting-in-alberta-1.2919975
117. DeClerq, K. (2014, June 27). *#obscurecdnlaws: What you need to know about Canadian law.* CTVNews. https://www.ctvnews.ca/mobile/canada/obscurecdnlaws-what-you-need-to-know-about-canadian-law-1.1889377
118. Zuber Brioux Blog. (2019, July 5). *6 of the most unusual laws in the world.* https://www.zuberbrioux.com/6-of-the-most-unusual-laws-in-the-world
119. Iverson, K. (2017, February 16). *A guide to Thailand's strange laws.* Culture Trip. https://theculturetrip.com/asia/thaila

nd/articles/a-guide-to-thailands-strange-laws

120. Payne, E. (2020, January 22). *Here are the countries where vaping is illegal or restricted including Thailand.* The Sun. https://www.thesun.co.uk/travel/4289492/countries-vaping-banned-explained
121. McDonald, J. (2020, February 25). *Mexico bans import of all vaping products, cites WHO guidance.* Vaping360. https://vaping360.com/vape-news/88831/mexico-bans-import-of-all-vaping-products-cites-who-guidance
122. Tripsavvy. (n.d.). *What is ley seca?* https://www.tripsavvy.com/what-is-ley-seca-1588853
123. Mowbray, S. (2017, August 15). *13 unusual laws in Switzerland even the Swiss don't know about.* Culture Trip. https://theculturetrip.com/europe/switzerland/articles/13-weird-swiss-laws-you-should-know-about
124. Burkhard, D. (2019, March 3). *Here are 11 Swiss "laws" that are weird and wacky.* Newly Swissed Online Magazine. https://www.newlyswissed.com/11-weird-swiss-laws
125. BBC News. (2011, November 17). *Swiss can ban naked hiking, court rules.* https://www.bbc.com/news/world-europe-15785219
126. Booth, S. (2018, October 12). *10 ridiculous Scottish laws you won't believe.* Scottish Field. https://www.scottishfield.co.uk/culture/10-ridiculous-scottish-laws-you-wont-believe
127. Barrington-Smith, T. (2018, July 30). *Forever hold your peace or face two years imprisonment.* Commercial Lore. https://commerciallore.com/2018/07/31/forever-hold-your-peace-or-face-two-years-imprisonment
128. Makela, M. (n.d.). *Weird Australian 'Laws' - Fact or fiction?* Go To Court Lawyers. https://www.gotocourt.com.au/leg

al-news/weird-australian-laws

129. Velarde, O. (2018, March 26). *9 Sri Lankan laws foreigners should know about*. Culture Trip. https://theculturetrip.com/asia/sri-lanka/articles/9-sri-lankan-laws-foreigners-should-know-about
130. SmartTraveller. (n.d.). *Covid-19 and travel.* https://www.smartraveller.gov.au/destinations/asia/sri-lanka
131. BBC News. (2014, April 22). *Sri Lanka to deport Buddha tattoo British woman.* https://www.bbc.com/news/world-asia-27107857
132. Roberts, R. (2020, February 16). *Photography laws in Dubai and the UAE*. ExpatWoman. https://www.expatwoman.com/dubai/money-finance/finance/photography-laws-in-dubai-and-uae
133. Travel Centre. (n.d.). *Morocco customs, currency & airport tax regulations details*. IATA. https://www.iatatravelcentre.com/MA-Morocco-customs-currency-airport-tax-regulations-details.htm
134. Williams, S. (2017, June 15). *Bizarre ways to get arrested in Morocco*. Culture Trip. https://theculturetrip.com/africa/morocco/articles/8-moroccan-laws-foreigners-will-find-unusual
135. Gauld, L. (2020, February 16). *Which countries have banned drones in 2020*. The Silver Nomad. https://www.thesilvernomad.co.uk/countries-that-have-banned-drones
136. Orbitz. (2017, December 6). *7 totally weird ways to get arrested in Europe*. HuffPost. https://www.huffpost.com/entry/7-totally-weird-ways-to-get-arrested-in-europe_b_7172920
137. Dinuzzo, E. (2017, July 27). *22 bizarre things you didn't know were banned or illegal around the world*. The Independent.

https://www.independent.co.uk/life-style/christmas/travel/22-bizarre-things-you-didn-t-know-were-banned-or-illegal-around-world-a7863111.html

138. Time Out Tokyo. (2015, August 18). *Top 10 strange laws in Japan.* https://www.timeout.com/tokyo/blog/top-10-strange-laws-in-japan-081815
139. Buerk, R. (2012, May 18). *Fugu: The Fish more poisonous than cyanide.* BBC News. https://www.bbc.com/news/magazine-18065372
140. Friedman, M. (2010, February 22). *Top 10 most dangerous foods.* TIME. https://content.time.com/time/specials/packages/article/0,28804,1967235_1967238_1967227,00.html
141. Wikipedia. (2016, May 31). *Salmon act 1986.* https://en.wikipedia.org/wiki/Salmon_Act_1986
142. Msinha. (2018, July 15). *It's illegal to name a pig Napoleon in France and other wacky laws.* The Sun. https://www.thesun.co.uk/news/6781852/its-illegal-to-name-a-pig-napoleon-in-france-and-other-wacky-laws
143. Natalie. (2019, July 5). *Strange laws you should know about in Paris.* Discover Walks Blog. https://www.discoverwalks.com/blog/strange-laws-you-should-know-about-in-paris
144. Sire, A. (2017, September 1). *No speedo? Then don't try to go swimming in France — seriously.* The World from PRX. https://www.pri.org/stories/2014-09-01/no-speedo-then-dont-try-go-swimming-france-seriously
145. Migan, J. (2017, October 9). *This one fact about France will challenge your idea of marriage.* Culture Trip. https://theculturetrip.com/europe/france/articles/this-one-fact-about-france-will-challenge-your-idea-of-marriage

146. Henter, M. (2019, November 15). *Cycling rules and fines in Denmark*. Expat Solutions. https://www.expatsolutions.dk/fines-for-breaking-cycling-rules
147. DISabroad. (n.d.). *The rules of the road...Biking like a Dane*. https://disabroad.org/wp-content/uploads/sites/4/2015/08/rules-tips-bike-like-a-dane-in-copenhagen-1.pdf
148. Israel, D. (2010, June 28). *8 countries with fascinating baby naming laws*. Mental Floss. https://www.mentalfloss.com/article/25034/8-countries-fascinating-baby-naming-laws
149. Martineau, A. (2015, January 4). *5 funny vacation stories & mishaps*. Go City. https://gocity.com/en-us/blog/travel-horror-stories-5-hilarious-vacation-mishaps
150. LeahciM, H. (2014, April 28). *30 people reveal their embarrassing moments because of a cultural misunderstanding*. Thought Catalog. https://thoughtcatalog.com/hok-leahcim/2014/04/30-people-reveal-their-embarrassing-moments-because-of-a-cultural-misunderstanding
151. Andrusaite, A. (2017, November 11). *15 incredibly funny and unusual travel adventure stories*. Reverie Chaser. https://reveriechaser.com/15-incredibly-funny-and-unusual-travel-adventure-stories
152. Ben551. (2019, December 2). *Funny hosting story that made my day*. Community Center. https://community.withairbnb.com/t5/Hosting/Funny-hosting-story-that-made-my-day/td-p/939403
153. Wong, V. (2017, September 22). *These crazy Airbnb stories will make you want to travel more*. Refinery29. https://www.refinery29.com/en-us/funny-airbnb-experiences-travel-stories#slide-2
154. Reader's Digest. (2020, September 12). *The funniest family*

vacations stories that you will sadly relate to. https://www.rd.com/list/vacation-stories

155. Deabler, A. (2020, February 17). *Bride claims groom's parents booked same hotel as couple's honeymoon spot.* Fox News. https://www.foxnews.com/lifestyle/bride-grooms-parents-same-hotel-honeymoon
156. Bowerman, M. (2015, November 17). *Dad films Vegas vacation, not realizing camera was in selfie mode.* USA TODAY. https://www.usatoday.com/story/news/nation-now/2015/11/17/dad-films-vegas-vacation-not-realizing-camera-selfie-mode/75914774
157. Dainius. (2015, October 30). *Passenger seated on plane next to stranger who looks exactly like him.* Bored Panda. https://www.boredpanda.com/bearded-men-lookalikes-doppelgangers-aeroplane-flight-neil-douglas-robert-stirling
158. Hostelgeeks. (2020, February 29). *Chickens, goats, and abba – the bizarre bus through Ethiopia.* https://hostelgeeks.com/chickens-goats-and-abba-the-bizarre-bus-through-ethiopia
159. SWI. (2018, November 28). *Why is Bern the capital of Switzerland?* https://www.swissinfo.ch/eng/-federal-city-_why-is-bern-the-capital-of-switzerland-/44577476
160. Wikipedia. (2001, December 6). *Brasilia.* https://en.wikipedia.org/wiki/Bras%C3%ADlia
161. Wikipedia. (2001, October 1). *Province of Canada.* https://en.wikipedia.org/wiki/Province_of_Canada
162. City of Ottawa. (n.d.). *A virtual exhibit: Ottawa becomes the capital.* https://ottawa.ca/en/arts-heritage-and-events/city-ottawa-archives/exhibitions-and-displays/virtual-exhibit-ottawa-becomes-capital

163. Wikipedia. (2001, November 3). *Wellington.* https://en.wikipedia.org/wiki/Wellington
164. Wikipedia. (2001, April 20). *Ankara.* https://en.wikipedia.org/wiki/Ankara
165. International Traveller. (2017, September 11). *10 global cities that seem like a capital – but they're not.* https://www.internationaltraveller.com/world/10-commonly-confused-capital-cities
166. Wikipedia. (2001, September 29). *South Africa.* https://en.wikipedia.org/wiki/South_Africa
167. Wikipedia. (2001, August 27). *Canberra.* https://en.wikipedia.org/wiki/Canberra
168. Wikipedia. (n.d.). *Melbourne.* McGill School Of Computer Science. https://www.cs.mcgill.ca/~rwest/wikispeedia/wpcd/wp/m/Melbourne.htm
169. Wikipedia. (2001, June 23). *Stendhal syndrome.* https://en.wikipedia.org/wiki/Stendhal_syndrome
170. Wikipedia. (2006, October 25). *Paris syndrome.* https://en.wikipedia.org/wiki/Paris_syndrome
171. Wikipedia. (2002, November 5). *Jerusalem syndrome.* https://en.wikipedia.org/wiki/Jerusalem_syndrome
172. SevenStreets. (n.d.). *7 strange city syndromes.* http://www.sevenstreets.com/seven-strange-city-syndromes
173. Nashawaty, C. (2012, February 17). *The Jerusalem syndrome: Why some religious tourists believe they are the Messiah.* Wired. https://www.wired.com/2012/02/ff-jerusalemsyndrome
174. Manickave, K. (2020, May 14). *Mythical or mystical? Revisiting India syndrome, which afflicts well-meaning, spirituality-seeking westerners.* Firstpost. https://www.firstpost.com/living/mythical-or-mystical-revisiting-india-syndrom

e-which-afflicts-well-meaning-spirituality-seeking-westerners-8344441.html

175. *Population by country (2021)*. (n.d.). Worldometer - real time world statistics. https://www.worldometers.info/world-population/population-by-country/
176. *Largest countries in the world by area*. (n.d.). Worldometer - real time world statistics. https://www.worldometers.info/geography/largest-countries-in-the-world/

Made in the USA
Monee, IL
24 March 2024

55697983R00056

Parallel Lives

Parallel Lives

Rita Harrison

Illustrated by Val Littlehales

A Child Cannot Know

A child who is battered and deprived,
Sees the world through haunted eyes,
She learns about mood swings, secrets and lies,
The must-have signals that help her survive.

A child cannot fight back or dare ask why
She has been given a whopping black eye,
Her pitiful sobs that lurch in the air
Meet with rejection from an ice cold stare.

Her hungry tummy is a different pain
And crying, the only way to complain
But often a fist is all that she tastes
Or a grimy pillow put over her face.

A child knows nothing of spliffs and booze,
The raw materials of her abuse.
Her wistful smile, lips pleading and thin,
Camouflages her fear within.

A child cannot know the reason why
She was born to parents who make her cry,
Or why she feels that she is to blame
For the every-day squalor splintered with shame.

Cover Design by Lars Rindsig
Illustrations by Val Littlehales

This first edition published in Great Britain in 2009 by
Four O'Clock Press—a Discovered Authors' imprint

ISBN 978-1-907136-06-1

Available from Discovered Authors Online—
All major online retailers and available to order through all UK bookshops

Or contact:

Books
Discovered Authors
Roslin Road, London
W3 8DH

0844 800 5214
books@discoveredauthors.co.uk
www.discoveredauthors.co.uk

Printed in the UK by BookForce Distribution
BookForce Distribution policy is to use papers that are natural, renewable
and recyclable products and made from wood grown in sustainable forests
wherever possible

BookForce Distribution Ltd.
Roslin Road, London
W3 8DH
www.bookforce.co.uk

Contents

Lily's Playground

I was born in a house in poverty lane
a clean, but humble abode,
my earliest memories still remain
of waiting for bombs to explode.

I played in the cemetery opposite,
unaware of ancestral bones,
and didn't think anything of it
as I played on the marble gravestones.

Whenever the sirens sounded,
I had to run quickly home
to hide in the air-raid shelter
which we prayed was a bomb-free zone.

It was cold and damp in the shelter
and everyone listened with fear
as doodlebugs dropped then fell silent,
we prayed they wouldn't land near.

When the siren signalled the all-clear,
   we emerged from the dark to the light,
alive and eternally grateful
   the invaders had been put to flight.

At last when the war was over,
   the shelter made an excellent den
where my pals played childish war games
   but I never went in it again.

Waiting for
bombs to
explode

Bernadette's Sanctuary

She was born in a house on comfort street,
to a family of well-to-do people
she played in a pretty walled garden
overlooked by the local church steeple.

Unaware of the girl in the cemetery,
she had everything money could buy,
descended from well-bred ancestry
her life was one long lullaby.

She liked rearranging her doll's house
and was always prettily dressed
playing make-believe in the summerhouse
with her tea-set and teddy as guest.

At the outbreak of war came some hardship
as Britain turned off all its lights,
and learned a lot about comradeship
when the men joined up for the fight.

With her family she hid in the cellar
which was furnished with all they required
and the stories her mamma would tell her
took her mind off the enemy's fire.

The war passed her by without drama,
not for her any traumas in store,
protected from thoughts that might harm her,
her charmed life was fully restored.

Not for her
any traumas
in store

The Wrong Daddy

I had never seen my daddy before
that night when he returned from the war,
Mummy hugged and kissed him and all that stuff
then he picked me up, his uniform felt rough.

I remember his moustache tickling my face
then his fingers touching me under my dress
I wriggled free, I knew he'd been brave
but was this how daddies were meant to behave?

The next time he touched me, I stiffened and knew
that something was wrong but what should I do?
Each night after that when he put me to bed
he said he'd tell stories, I was frightened instead.

He said not to tell or else he'd kill mummy
and that's when I got this pain in my tummy.
Sometimes I cried and he looked afraid
but his secret game was always played.

Pressed hard against me, hand on my mouth
I felt his hot breath, heard him shout
And when a noise on the stair made him aware,
he quickly told stories of Rupert Bear.

When mummy walked in, she never knew
what daddy was always making me do.
I have always wanted my very own dad
but now I've got him, I'm ever so sad.

Sometimes I cried
and he looked afraid

Bedtime Stories

Going to bed is always fun,
I'm usually there by seven thirty one.
Mostly I choose what dad must read,
he sits by my bed with the book on his knee.

I've lots of books about different things
but he likes reading, Lord of the Rings
which boys might like, but me it scares,
was that a noise I heard on the stairs?

I creep into mum's bed in the night,
shivering and cold from absolute fright,
my daddy wakes up and laughs at me
and mum lifts her head, drowsily.

Come along, little girl, back to sleep,
let's try counting those little white sheep,
says Daddy, tucking me into my bed
and planting a kiss on top of my head.

In the morning he says it's all right
about being scared in the middle of the night,
Mummy has promised to leave on a light
and dad will be reading me, Snow White.

Going to bed is always fun

In a 1940s Courtroom

I sat in the courtroom on an old man's knee,
the very last place I wanted to be
but he was a magistrate and he
was about to adjudicate the plea
regarding my daddy who stood accused
of something nasty, called abuse.

I sat very still, afraid to complain,
my eyes just level with the man's watch chain,
as he and two others spoke my name
in whispers, as though I were to blame
for my daddy behaving inappropriately
making me touch his thingammy.

I felt myself slipping off the old man's knee
he had a fat tummy and short legs, you see.
I managed to cling on nervously,
scared they might leave him alone with me,
and if they did, that he might also do
those things that grown-ups say are taboo.

The fat man said in a monotone,
This sort of thing must not be condoned,
then they spoke together in undertones,
She must be examined. Case postponed.
My mother was crying, it was all very sad,
my daddy had done something very bad.

The doctor who saw me was also a man
so I looked at the door and nearly ran,
when he looked at my parts, my tears began,
was it happening again, a new bogeyman?
I closed my eyes and counted to ten,
yes, it was happening all over again...

My eyes just level with
the man's watch chain

In the Albert Hall

When my special day arrived at last,
I washed and dressed myself really fast,
I was so excited I could hardly stand still,
receiving my prize would be such a thrill.

Mum and dad drove me to the Albert Hall,
a circular building I'd never seen before
And as we queued to get inside,
I saw their faces were filled with pride.

I was given a name tag and taken aside
and told where to stand at the end of a line,
Then in came the princess dressed all in green,
the most beautiful lady I'd ever seen.

Slowly she moved along the row,
bending forward, each medal to bestow;
rewards for children who had done brave deeds
like helping others in their hour of need.

When my turn came I blushed bright red,
You're a very brave girl, Bernadette, she said.
I looked at my medal and was really glad
I'd been able to revive my unconscious dad.

Then in came the
Princess dressed
all in green

50th

Suffer the Little Children

(Morning assembly in a 1950s Grammar School)

In morning assembly,
as we closed our eyes and prayed,
while chanting The Commandments,
I always felt betrayed;
and when we said, The Lord's Prayer,
I found that I would rather
never say those two words, Our Father,
because, if He were really up there
looking down on me,
surely He could see *my* father's cruelty.

Honour thy father and thy mother
the fifth Commandment reads
I thought there should have been another
to meet abused kids' needs.
Yet there's no eleventh Commandment
banning sexual embezzlement
of children who are helpless to complain
about their secret lives of shame.

In morning assembly, I always felt unreal,
compared with other girls, my life surreal,
but filing back to class in our crocodile,
I always managed a stitched-on-smile
so no-one ever knew the truth,
my father's sin had stripped me of my youth.

(*Our secret*, he said. But I owned the pain.)

With Childline no invention,
and no Heavenly intervention,
I asked myself,
was God the Father really there,
witnessing my pain?

And then,   I never prayed again.

My father's sin had
stripped me of my youth

The Prefect's Prayer

Familiar faces,
Some she could name,
Pretty girls, plain girls,
Each day the same.

Bernadette, the prefect in charge,
Ushered them in to their symbolic Ark,
The assembly hall
Where prayers would begin,
Saving their souls from drowning in sin.

When heads were bowed in supplication,
The prefect glanced round the congregation;
There stood the sad girl near the door,
Gaze averted to the floor,
Head bowed in silent despair
As others recited the Lord's Prayer.

Our Father, the prefect said,
Then whispered these words instead,

Dear Lord,
See the young girl, over there?
The one who shuns the Lord's Prayer,
Whose head is bowed as in disgrace,
Please take her in to Your embrace
And lift the sad look from her face.
I shall try to be her friend
And hope one day she'll pray again.
Thank you Lord.

Amen.

I Am the Child

I am the child
standing alone in the playground,
watching other kids
and the boisterous games they play,
their shouts competing
with my sad thoughts of the day.

I am the child
who sits at the back of the class,
my mind on my bruises,
not the lesson of the day.

When the teacher questions me,
I am unable to say.

I am the child
excused from all games,
asthmatic they think but
cigarette burns are hidden away.
It's no fun being me, it's no child's play.

My mind
on my bruises

Teacher's Pet

But in my school
there's one girl in particular
who stands perpendicular,
she has long golden hair
and personality to spare;
in the middle of a crowd,
she's always there.

In the playground
it's a leadership thing,
we are her puppets
and she pulls our strings,
she decides if we play tag or skip
and meekly, we follow her leadership

She always sits at the front of the class
and is never afraid of being asked
she knows all the answers, rat, tat, tat,
quick as a flash, just like that,
she's an intellectual acrobat.

She's never, ever, at a loose end
because everyone wants to be her friend;
she's captain of this and leader of that
she really is one cool cat.
No wonder tall, blonde, Bernadette,
has so much fun being teacher's pet.

We are her puppets

The Latch Key Kid

I turn the key in the lock,
let myself in,
hear the tick of the clock.

Beware!
Sin hangs in the air.

A tap drips,
a floor creaks,
I count the sounds
slicing the atmosphere.

This latch key kid
is on intimate terms with fear.

My skin is waxy with adrenalin
my courage, only wafer-thin.

With doll-like jerks I creep about,
hold my breath,
and then the threat...
The step on the stair!
Beware!
The gingerbread man hovers there.

He is the cat,
I am the mouse
I am fast but he can pounce
to take advantage of my vulnerability;
not enough he stole my virginity.
This gingerbread, figurehead of respectability...

I have cried carpets of tears
but now, instead, I whistle in my head.

On intimate terms with fear

Home for Tea

Teacher caught me drifting
in the middle of last lesson.

Dreaming of the home bell
and how I'll soon be running,
hell for leather down our street,
my mum there to greet me,
pinny on, maybe curlers in her hair
but so what?
At least she'll be there.

The house will be warm,
a smell of baking in the air,
I'll give mum a hug
throw my bag on the stairs,
tease her a bit
about the metal in her hair.

I love these times after school
just me and our mum, as a rule,
Then my dad comes home,
throws his coat on the chair,
kisses mum, tousles my hair.

Then it's homework time
and I'll be off to my room
'til dinner's dished up.
After that,
dad and I will do the washing up.

Great!

I love these times after school

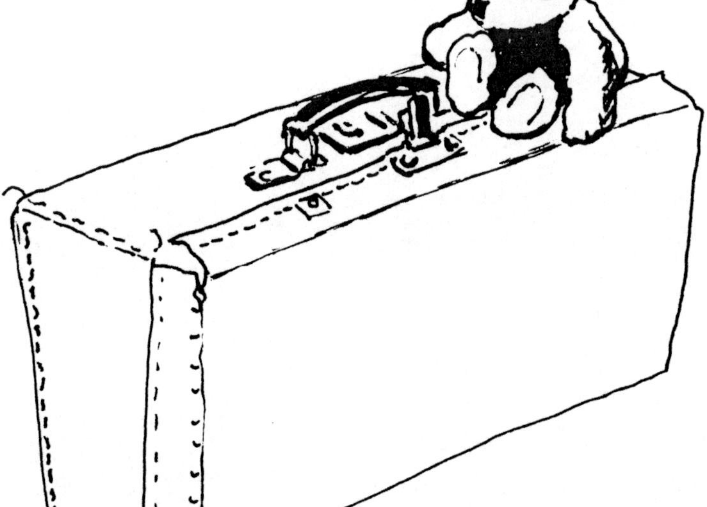

The Fostering

The door squeaked open
letting in the sun
and other awkward people,
none of them my mum.
Each time that door opened
I wished it would be her
coming in, last minute,
to stop this transfer.

The room was small and dusty
and we sat on wobbly chairs,
me and the foster folk
who said I would be theirs
if mum didn't come and get me
before the forms were signed,
but little chance of that,
in her state of mind.

An inner door opened
and we were led inside,
and a panel of three people,
all beady-eyed,
asked us our names
and lots of other questions,
I knew that my future
lay at their discretion,
and, limp as a rag doll,
I was lost in depression.

The court was told my mother
didn't want me anymore.
Still, I kept my fingers crossed
as I watched the door,
but after some discussion
the papers were all signed,
no longer would I live with mum,
instead I'd been assigned
to a different kind of misery,
I was about to find.

I adapted to my new life,
I really had no option
but to learn the unfair rules
of my new adoption,
I became the other woman
when I was just fifteen,
advantages were taken
that were quite obscene.

When that door squeaked open,
letting in the sun
and other awkward people,
it should have been my mum...

My mother
didn't want me
any more

The Family

Through a door left ajar
I heard mum and dad talking
about something called war.

Mum was crying and
saying things like bombs and dying
and dad was trying to comfort her.

I was a little bit scared
and then a lot more
when, I saw the suitcase by the door
and my teddy sitting on it.

Mum took off her pinny
and put on her hat,
sat me down and explained to me that
I was going with other girls and boys
to stay in the country
away from the danger,
but I didn't want to live with a stranger.

As I got on the bus for our journey
and waved down at the mums and dads
I could see that mine were unhappy
and I was ever so sad.

Then as we were all being counted
my mum climbed into the bus,
Bernadette, come on, she shouted,
You're coming back home with us.
This family will stay together,
there's nothing more to discuss.

This family will stay together

In his Image

When I was young and life was grim,
My mother kept saying,
You're the image of 'im;
'im's my absent father, full of sin.

There was no mirror so I could not see
That in his likeness there was me,
I looked at my sister who looked like our mum
And I wished it was her who looked like 'im.

My face was a burden all my young life,
Having his likeness, caused me such strife,
Why did my mother keep saying such things
Making me feel I'd committed a sin,
When I couldn't help looking like 'im?

There was no mirror
so I could not see

Daddy's Girl

My mother called me her little princess
And smiled as she spoke with tenderness,
You once had a daddy, as handsome as can be
And you get your looks from him, not plain old me.

She showed me his picture so I could see
That I looked like my daddy and he looked like me,
He had a lovely smile and I felt really glad
That mummy was right, I did look like my dad.

You get your looks
from him

Dealing with the Skeletons

Then I grew up and, what did I find?
Sleepless nights,
hell crouching in corners of my mind
where phobias found places to hide.

Life without structure, leading me where?
Journeys to work,
distant screams following me there.
I am the jobless waitress, usherette,
night time shelf-filler,
stacking foods priced way beyond my means,
always dreaming my cellotaped dreams.

I longed to lead a normal life.
I wanted, what? To be someone's wife.
So I sought direction of a professional kind
I invited a therapist into my mind.

LIMITED PERFORMANCES/MUST END SOON

Having cast me in the Juvenile Lead,
he raised the safety curtain,
and gave me the five minute call...

ACT I

Scene—*A small, shabby living room*

I spoke on cue, shocked by the voice
of the child I still carried in my heart.
I am hiding under the table,
mum's lying beaten on the floor
I want to be invisible
no more games, please, no more.
Now he's dragging me away,
and I want to stay with mummy
please let me stay.

ACT II

Scene—*Same room three years later*

I had to tell. They took him away.
Left mum with a child on the way.
We lived in poverty marinated in shame,
that's when mum took him back again.
I was thirteen then and old enough to know
that, this time, I just couldn't tell.
Couldn't put my mum through more hell...

At this point, the clock-faced stranger gave
no review, except to say our time was through.
But after quite a long run I took my bow.
Nightmares gone, unbroken sleep now.

In time I became aware of a new leading man
standing there, in the wings, with a happier script;
a romantic two-parter about how to commit.

Inspired Success

I'm an ash blonde sophisticate
with a clutch of certificates
and trophies for sport of every kind,
I have two point four kids,
hold three directorships,
his and her Bentleys
side by side on the drive
and friends who drop in
for drinks, pool side.

I'm a local JP with an MBE
for charity work with the NSPCC,
I was inspired by a girl
in school, I once knew.

Until I met Lily, child abuse
meant a slap on the wrist,
or a clip round the ear.
Oh, I heard the whisperings,
but I had no idea
until I befriended her
after assembly one day.

Sad and alone,
she told me she couldn't go home.
And why!
I was shocked but what could I say
about the extra lesson I learned that day.

And then she was gone.
No-one knew where; most didn't care.
But I couldn't get her out of my mind.
Naively I'd thought her the only one
then I learned there were others
and knew something must be done.
I wanted to make their lives
less of a disaster.

I wanted to feed them
silver spoonfuls of laughter.

I heard the
whisperings

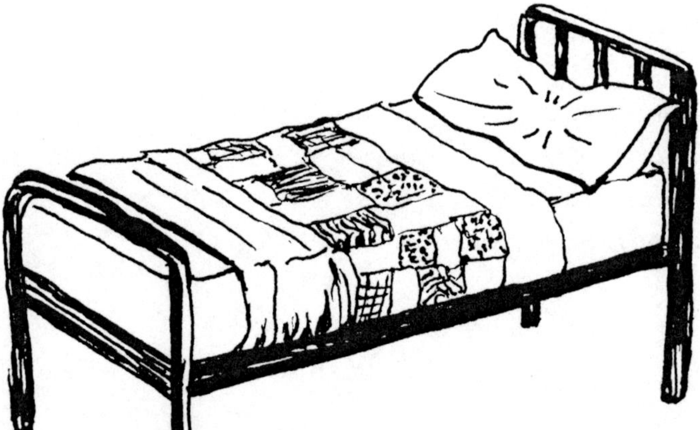

Lily's Nightmare

Is that you, Reg?
Ssh, now, old lady, the male nurse replied.
Yes I'm your Reg come to lie by your side.

But it's dark now, something's not right,
No visits are allowed in the night.

Hush now, old lady, you're so like a child,
I'm your Reg, remember? Said the paedophile,
Come to lie with you for a little while.

§

Sleep well did you, Lily?
Teased the day nurse, amused,
Unsuspecting of any abuse
Of the old girl who insisted
That her Reg, despite being dead,
Came creeping each night, into her bed.
You imagine your Reg comes to your bed
It's a lot of old nonsense filling your head,
The memory plays tricks the older we get.

Poor Lily lay silent, old and confused,
That her gentle Reg had left her so bruised.

And that paedophile nurse was never accused.

Peace Haven

I've booked myself into this rest home,
expensive, but I've income of my own.
My old, lacy bones are inclined to break,
so the move was best for everyone's sake.
I have my privacy when I close the door
to my private room with its chintz décor.

Absentee energy, good works all done,
Now I'm content to let the young carry on.
These are halcyon days when a bell rings at four
and I join others for tea and a little rapport.

My family do come to take me out,
but widowhood and old age
are nothing to shout about.
Best to ignore one's aches and pains
and take into account the many gains
like how staff are kind and how one may
sleep soundly at night, with peace of mind.

Some homes for the elderly
can be quite hateful, or so I am told,
but Peace Haven is an excellent home for the old.

napac

The National Association for People Abused in Childhood was established for survivors, by survivors.

Research reveals that 10% of children suffer from some form of abuse—physical, sexual or emotional. The legacy—splintered personalities, traumatised emotions—leaves the victims struggling to come to terms with life's challenges. Because, for the most part, the scars are not visible, there is insufficient recognition of the need to help victims.

Recovery is often delayed because victims have been schooled into keeping the abuse secret. The burden of that secrecy takes its toll in many painful ways.

NAPAC's mission is to encourage people to take control of their healing. Recovery begins when they discover that others care. The freedom to talk to someone when the need arises is vital. NAPAC's trained volunteers provide the listening ears.

To fulfil its mission, NAPAC needs money and volunteers to respond to over a thousand weekly telephone calls for help.

Freephone support line: 0800 085 3330

www.napac.org.uk

NAPAC, 42 Curtain Road, London EC2A 3NH
NAPAC is a registered charity (No. 1069802)